The Secret Code To

Success And Wealth

In Online Business

Genevieve-Gold Flight

For Reseller information, including discounts and premium sales, please call our sales team on +447562642826. For Press review copies, Author interviews, or other publicity information, please contact us on +447562642826 or email – info@goldventureslimited.com .

Special discounts are available on quantity buys by corporations, associations, charities, philanthropists and other individuals. For details, contact the publisher at the Email address above or by Phone.

Follow on Twitter

@SCode2OnlineBiz ‖ @Genevieveflight

ISBN: 1479341967

ISBN13: 978-1479341962

Kindle eBook: B00BCMTBJ6

Dedication

I would like to dedicate this book to my very loving mum, Late Beatrice Ego Ndukwe (Nee Ndionu) whose beautiful soul and gentle nature inspired me immensely and taught me a lot about the true meaning of life, and the need to help and inspire others in every little way we can.

CONTENTS

Author's Acknowledgements

This book has evolved over a time. During the slow and often interrupted evolution of this book, I came to learn a lot and of course passed through so many challenges which I have the space to acknowledge here. All those challenges were able to strengthen and inspire me towards achieving my desire in life and pursuing a fulfilling life destiny.

Participation in so many business events, webinars, conferences and trainings were intellectually stimulating as these opportunities helped me to understand Business and Online Business in a global perspective. It enabled me to work together with many experts in diverse fields, visit many new places around the World, learn new things and most importantly it shaped my thoughts in a way that has helped me to accomplish my desire of becoming a Published Author.

I have been deeply inspired by many transformational leaders and role models. I would like to specially mention the following; President Barack Obama, Robert Kiyosaki, Raymond Aaron, Bill Walsh, Michelle Obama, Oprah Winfrey, Dr Farrah Gray, Chuka Umunna MP, Brian Tracy, and Anthony Robbins.

Other transformational leaders that have inspired me in life include Sir Richard Branson, James Caan, Lord Sugar, Les Brown, T. Harv Eker, Stedman Graham, Karren Brady, Don Lemon CNN, Andy Harrington, Connie Ragen Green, James

Lafferty, Jon Snow, Saj P, Niurka, Aliko Dangote, Ngozi Okonjo-Iweala, Vic Conant, and many others.

Special thanks to a great friend of mine Chan, whose advice and immense support has been very highly inspiring.

My special thanks to my Dad, Hon Basil Ndukwe for his immense support.

To my family and extended family members, thanks for all your best wishes and support.

To all my Rotarian friends and Colleagues from all over the World, thanks for the opportunity of working with you all. To all my friends on Social Networks, you all made the corners of the world appear so near to me.

To everyone that has helped me along the way, my thanks go to you all for the joy and positive spirit you brought into my life.

Introduction

Many times, many people do ask whether it is feasible to get started in online business and at the same time earn a decent living with it. Absolutely! Time spent diligently investigating the numerous opportunities, and learning the abilities of effective online business owners, will certainly spare you from making pricey blunders.

Have you ever before considered the possibility of operating your own online business? An increasing number of individuals are now depending on the power of the internet to create or offer solutions or items to others. Online Businesses or Home based businesses are becoming increasingly lucrative in appeal today. Perhaps it's also time for you to consider how to become an online business owner with your very own home based business. If you have a family, it can be extremely challenging to manage your time in between a normal career and family life. This is not the end of the world for you as when you're at home and taking care of your family members, you could likewise be running an online business. Very often, if only the husband or the wife is working, the earnings are inadequate to meet up with the family needs. The money you could make from your online business may be a real lifesaver while at the same time enabling you to have all those additional things that can make life fun. In the current economic environment and with additional redundancies in the headlines each day, there has never ever been a much better time to start an online business or home based business.

The difficulty is in selecting the right business for you. There are several online business possibilities to choose from. You need to look for the real precious stones among all the jewels. It will certainly take time checking out the numerous online business opportunities and deciding on the correct one that will function for you. That's why this publication "The Secret Code To Success And Wealth™ In Online Business" has been created for you. You might additionally have to develop a different mindset. Operating your very own business calls for an incredibly separate state of mind to being an employee. That's a fact. These are all capabilities or skills that could be learned by anyone.

Nobody is born to be a business man or woman. It only takes a great thinker to create a genius idea that can transform into a successful business model. If you have, or may establish the top qualities of an entrepreneur, an online business or home based business may be the answer to your financial freedom. If you have your very own personal Computer and most significantly, an Internet connection, you may effortlessly become a business owner who owns or operates an online business. You have to also see to it that the business is legitimate to stay off any type of issues that could arise in the future. There are several valid "business" models you can easily follow. Social media has provided so many options today and comes in quite handy. The first option could be to become an Affiliate marketer. For those who are limited in the resources they may use for their brand-new business, this is an excellent selection. You may or may not need a small amount of cash to get started. You will have to find an affiliate company that will certainly give you various services or items to start with. You don't always require your own website to start as an Affiliate marketer.

All you have to do is to direct consumers to the main affiliate website. Your referral payment will usually be made once you reach the least payment threshold. You will usually receive percentages for every product offered or for the services provided. If you prefer to have a larger market, you could transform your home based business into an online business. One of the beautiful things about the internet is that your customer base is extremely global.

Ultimately, any Online Business model you do choose may take a great deal of work, particularly if you're just beginning. You will certainly have to know how to market your online business and find all the capabilities required to operating it effectively. There are literally hundreds of opportunities when it comes to running an online business. By searching on the internet, you can easily find the right business opportunity that will be ideal for you. If you invest time nurturing yourself as an entrepreneur, you will certainly be assured that your initiatives will not be in vain if you engage in your very own online business. Learn the capabilities and select your option wisely and you will surely succeed.

Doing an online business can effortlessly be a great opportunity for you. Nonetheless, an online business will certainly require great willpower. It is extremely simple and easy to educate yourself that you need to focus on the online business you want to create and that means you will definitely need to discipline yourself by remaining very focused to achieve your goal. This obviously will mean following a specific strategy that will guide you to success. It is always good to check how your rivals are prospering in their online business using different avenues including social media. Your online business can easily compete with the considerable significant brands when it pertains to social media, so figure out exactly what's currently generating revenue for them. That you started an online business does not mean that you are above looking for ways to construct and sustain desirable customer partnerships. Failure to act as expected could easily lead to customer dissatisfaction and could effectively affect your business and the trusting relationship your business deserves in the online business world. You might want to believe that as an online business owner, you have to do everything on your own and that's not typically the case. There are many places that you could conveniently uncover certified, cost-effective help for whatever task you need done. Always keep in contact with your customers to improve areas where your business might be lacking in customer satisfaction. This will certainly assist you in enhancing your online business and you could simply also use the testimonials received from your customers to create a brand-new segment of your website entitled 'customer reviews'. Always seek unbiased opinions along with using the greatest ones on the website. Pay yourself a salary along with spending revenue towards creating quality in your online business. It can be tempting when you start generating decent income from your online business, nevertheless always work like an expert in your field along with spending any sort of additional money into the business. This will certainly assist your online business to expand even further. Taking the plunge into an online business can often seem to be a daunting chore, however by organizing yourself and stepping forward, you will have more chance for success. The extremely first thing you really should do is to take time, and write out a step by step plan for how you can easily implement your online business. This will definitely assist you in recognizing exactly what needs to be done to follow your plan and goal. Ideally, you have studied a bit more about starting your own home based online business. You have to be able to recognize all the hurdles that you are likely going to have to leap over. Simply remember, starting out is exceedingly difficult. However, study as repeatedly as you can so that you are all set for any roadblocks that will unavoidably pop up in this brand-new undertaking.

How This Book Is Organized

This book comes in eleven chapters, having been strategically organized using DiaMonD GiFT™ Technique.

Chapters 1, 2, and 3 will cover how to get started by finding a specific, focused niche, how to integrate social media and attract customers.

Chapters 4, 5, and 6 will cover marketing through branding, search engine optimization and how to make it all legal.

Chapter 7 will extensively cover great websites, some of which are "underground," which successful millionaires use extensively to succeed in online business.

Chapters 8, 9, 10, and 11 will cover the latest tools and strategies that will help your online business succeed, other ways to promote your business, Facebook for business and ten steps to becoming a successful online entrepreneur.

Chapter 1
Diving In and Starting Your Online Business

In This Chapter

Is There an Existing Need in the Market?

Discovering What is Available Using Google Trends & Keyword Tools

Researching on Your Niche Products

Creating a Business Plan, Setting Goals and Budget

Designing a Well Secured Professional Website

Why You Cannot Afford to Neglect Data Backup

Integrating Payment Processing Systems

Optimizing for Search Engines to Find Your Business

Advertising and Promoting Your Business Website

Is There an Existing Need in the Market?

Today's world economy leaves little doubt about the fact that gone are the days when people have to rely on finding a job which entails working for somebody else as a solution to their financial problem or the only means to earning a living. If you want a chance to retire well, pay off debt and have any level of financial freedom, you need to be working for yourself. You are either working for yourself; building your future and your destiny or you are working for someone else, therefore building their own future or destiny. Which one would you prefer? We have all seen how far we can go when working for somebody else as you can never get rich working for somebody else. Today, it's every man and woman for themselves. The irony is that the current economic situation together with social media created many opportunities for you than ever existed before. When you combine the current economic situations and everyday basic needs which entails that an average person has to make an extra income or better still generate a steady level of multiple cash flow to move a step further that could help towards the possibility of enjoying financial freedom. With the global reach of the Internet, you have an unprecedented situation and starting an online business is actually the best thing for you to do right now. People all over the world are looking for work and using the internet to reach literally billions of people worldwide with your offer of help cannot be under estimated. If you know how to take advantage of this opportunity by starting an online business, it is immensely powerful and lucrative. The key of course is also finding the right online business and that's why this book has been written to show you the right places and strategies.

Happily, there is a way you can choose an online business that will fit you like a glove. Because finding a business that will help you succeed should be a priority to you, there are things that you must consider before you align yourself with any particular online business model. If you find a business that meets only three of the five benchmarks below I presume you will be also prosperous and happy. It is vital that if you find a company or online business that meets some standards, you will have found a home. A business you could be proud of, that will reward you beyond what you can even consider possible today, and one that you can share with others who need help in those areas of business. Creating financial freedom for yourself and helping others at the same time is definitely a win-win situation and nothing could be better than that. Let's take a look at the five focused denominators of a successful online business.

Find a True Leader in Your Targeted Niche: You can easily research online to find market leaders in specific fields and see what they are doing to succeed and learn from them.

Is There a Proven System? For beginners, it is very important that when you want to select a market leader to follow, it is essential to ensure that your chosen market leader has created a system that can guide you through to success. You want to make sure the system they offer you can be used by both beginners and people with more advanced knowledge.

Finding the Right Team to Help You Succeed: Working for yourself should not mean working on your own. The last thing you need is an online business that requires you to be up and awake at all hours of the day and night punching your keyboard. Another thing to look for within the team is whether there will be a mentor to guide you. Being assigned to a team of like-minded people will be key in your success. You will have questions and will surely need support.

Take a Sudden Leap of Faith: Once you finally decide you will like to start an online business, choose an ideal niche you will prefer to focus on and move decisively in that direction. In other words, you will plan to start right away and get involved now, rather than later. You can always look for a company or companies that can possibly do everything you need to do online for your business and chapter seven of this book will cover many important "underground" websites and businesses that more than 95% of online business owners use to succeed online today. Remember, you are establishing your own online business. Therefore you have to make sure that the company can sign you up online and that you can have immediate access to all the tools you will need to get started right away.

Does the Business Have a Global Reach? If the company you are considering can't do business all over the world then keep searching. By this I do not mean having offices all over the world but rather I mean that the most powerful part of doing business online is that people can buy from your business 24 hours a day, seven days a week from any location around the world. Remember that when you align yourself with a particular niche or company, you are doing more than just "joining up." You are giving them the most valuable gift they will ever get; your time and your passion. If you find a company that meets three or more of the criteria above or if you find one that meets all five, sign up to them as always free to do so and work your way to success in online business. Many individuals today have a work-at-home business enterprise success stories. Perhaps you too will one day become the next success story. As earlier said and to clarify again, you are either working for yourself, building your future and your destiny or you are working for someone else, therefore building their own future or their own destiny. The last thing you need is an online business that requires you to be up at all hours of the day and night punching your keyboard. You can always look for a company that can possibly do everything you need to do online and chapter seven will cover many important websites and businesses that online business owners use to succeed online. You are in the process of establishing your own online business. Make sure the company can sign you up online and that you can have immediate access to all the tools you will need to get started right away.

Discovering What is Available Using Google Trends and Keyword Tools

Google Trends: <u>Google Trends</u> is a remarkable tool that has quickly become indispensable to online business owners, online marketers, bloggers, information lovers and curious people. As the globe's most prominent search engine and one of the steering pressures behind the continued development of the internet, Google's position on the internet world is undeniably that of a trendsetter. While Google may strongly influence the direction in which the internet profits, its self-professed devotion to making details much more obtainable for individuals around the world means it likewise pays close attention to global trends in search. The huge amount of data it gathers on search frequencies has been collated into the daily updated Google Trends, a lead-in solution that has easily become crucial to online marketers, bloggers, data lovers and interested people.

<u>Google Trends</u> is a basic yet incredibly practical device that shows the search volume for a particular keyword since 2004 on a twin axis chart. This is labeled the Search Quantity Index graph. Alongside this is the Updates Reference Amount chart, which is specifically useful when analyzing just how the search volume associated with a specific term aligns with its popularity on various websites. The value of this setup is neatly demonstrated by the effects it has on

some search terms for example "flight." Throughout time, the search volume for "flight" follows greatly the same design, increasing in January after the Christmas and New Year break previously dipping and climbing again in the summer season. While the January surge in "flight" search quantity is mapped on Google Trends' chart, there is another considerably greater increase in April. This spike is mirrored in the News Reference volume graph, which shows a massive increase in newspaper articles having the word "flight." The opportunities are never-ending when it comes to tracking emerging trends in the market. You ought to considerably use them in your online business. Specifying Google alerts for brand-new items, services or emerging innovations will definitely be the best thing to do to keep track of new opportunities in the online business world. There are other methods you can easily use to monitor existing trends in the market. The core idea of leveraging a significant opportunity exists when a new item is launched online. The only method to use and do that is to be on as several Joint Venture (JV) lists as possible and to be there when any online marketer requires new members to join them. To start doing this, you can visit websites like the Warrior Forum or the Digital Point Forums and make yourself known by participating in the forums. You could become an affiliate with other internet online marketers and begin selling their products and they will certainly notify you of new products coming into the internet market. Furthermore, you ought to be actively participating in every significant forum or network you can easily locate. The only true means to being aware of these trends in the market is to be on the mailing lists of individuals you wish to work with. That needs cautious analysis and an understanding of your particular niche which will certainly take weeks otherwise months to obtain. To link up with Internet marketers, you need to sign up to their mailing list. This will help you to keep track of new developments in their respective businesses and this will surely guarantee you are plugged into those opportunities. It is also important to have a virtual assistant that will be able to track your Google Alerts and check your list subscriptions. The Headlines Recommendation Volume chart has constantly been essential in helping online search engine optimization experts that are making use of Google Trends to distinguish between normal spikes in search volume and those that are created by a popular newspaper article. These two graphs aren't the only devices being used by Google Trends. Google trends homepage hosts an hourly updated listing of the leading 10 "Hot Searches" in the USA, which is inevitably dominated by sports components and entertainment tales as well as key phrases from updated headlines. Showed along with visual information are the local variations in search volume for specified term, as well as the foreign languages in which it is most famously been browsed. Most interestingly for search advertising professionals, especially those who are new to the industry - Google Trends enables you to compare search volume for many terms at the same time, by comparing the results side-by-side on the same graph. For example, a search for "Obama, flight" displays the recorded search volumes for these two prominent search terms all at once, revealing that "Obama" continually eclipsed the search volume for "flight" though both were about equivalent at the same time.

Google Keyword Tool: Google keyword tool is one of many keyword tools that you may use when searching for keywords. What Google Keyword tool does is that it decides upon different keyword phrases that individuals typically browse for. There are global monthly searches, local monthly searches, and it also shows the search trends. It reveals the number of times individuals have entered a specific keyword phrase in Google's Search Engines. Remember this device is created for people to make use of for Google AdWords, which is Google's pay per click (PPC) service. This is set up to reveal how much competitors there is for a particular keyword so that you will know if you would like to use them and how much you would have to pay to use them. Using Google Keyword tool is merely a general guide, however it is incredibly practical. There are various other sites and programs you can easily use to do similar study. It would not help you if you focus your energy in finding the perfect keywords. You can invest much time doing this and it might not be the greatest use of your time. Some people and companies take this search to the extreme but I believe that it is more important to see to it that your keywords explain your business efficiently, than to obtain the most preferred keywords. What you should be interested in is turning website traffic into profit for your online business. You may use key phrases that are used in a great deal of searches, however if they do not concentrate on exactly what your online business is offering, you may not be able to receive targeted web traffic to your website which will be able to convert into leads to enable you sell your online products or attract more customers. By getting a high amount of traffic to your website using even more targeted keywords, you will certainly have a considerably better chance of converting them into paying clients, given that they will probably be a lot more curious about your product. It is additionally important that you research on your keyword while you are building your website to ensure that you can do the online search engine optimization (SEO) alongside developing your website. This could be done by searching for the right keywords using Google trends, Google keyword tools as well as also by getting the right domain name URL associated with the specific keyword you want to be ranked for. Always ensure that your website content includes relevant content that contains precisely what your website is going to be used for. For Instance, you would not want to have a website for dog food on your website when you want to focus on eBay for dummies. As you can see both do not match up with each other.

Researching on your Niche products

When you are creating a website which you intend to use to generate streams of income in your online business, one of the most crucial facts is that you certainly need to discover a specific niche in which you could operate comfortably. Naturally, finding a specific niche you want to concentrate on is not all that challenging, however locating a niche that is really successful could be a whole lot tougher especially if you are just a beginner. The first trick to discovering a lucrative niche that is specific to your needs is finding out something that people are most likely to be looking for online, and the second secret to finding a rewarding specific niche is selecting a particular niche that is not so competitive that you will be capable of making money from it. There are 4 specific tools that will help you to discover products that are of broader interest to people searching to buy online. The initial tool is eBay Pulse. By using eBay pulse, you will see exactly what the most preferred searches are, the most preferred stores, and the most-watched items are on eBay!

With this information, you will certainly have a better understanding of what people are buying, which will offer you a few ideas of particular niches to target. The second tool is Amazon. By going to "Store all divisions" on Amazon, you will be able to click on the significant groups Amazon lists and see just what Amazon has included on the front page of each category. You may be amazed at a few of the products you discover and may be even more astounded at just how quickly you could make money by developing sites that focus on these items.

The Google Keyword tool is the third device you should use to discover a profitable specific niche, as you could see just what words, terms, and products are most searched by customers, which will offer you a better concept of where you ought to focus your efforts. The last is Google trends which we covered in the previous page. When you find a niche you want to focus on, the next step is very straightforward. You just need to narrow down your search from a basic product to a particular item and use buyer keywords to attract customers to your site, and watch as your income from this website steadily climbs. Discovering a rewarding Specific niche does not need to be painful. Clickbank offers some tools that can assist in speeding up the process of locating a specific niche for you as the products on their website are categorized according to niches and are additionally rated according to different sale degrees including popularity, gravity, average sale, marketplace rating, percentage sale and the like. All you need to do is sign up with them and pick up the link for an item to market to your targeted audience. Among the best methods of making money online is to target a particular niche market which is an understanding that leads many individuals to speculate exactly what they may do to get much better conversions for a specific niche. However if you are wishing to be successful with niche advertising in your online business, you will need to ensure that you are not placing the cart before the horse. People usually get inside the bad habit of choosing a specific niche and "becoming married to it" and battering their head against it all trying to figure out exactly how they could optimize their success within that niche, and falling short to recognize that there are many other specific niches out there to pick from. To get much better targeted niche leads, do your due diligence to figure out which specific niches are much more likely to produce positive cash flow for your online business. Instead of selecting a niche and wishing you can easily press some excellent leads out of it, get information on all the particular niches that will certainly afford you the chance for good income.

Once you have this list on hand, you will certainly be able to shorten the options to the particular niches you feel relaxed exploring, and could then take the time to discover which of these particular niches are probably going to yield better outcomes. When you have done searching for potentially profitable niche leads, and introducing your online business from this initial pointer, you could create an online business that will certainly be both satisfying and lucrative, as opposed to being stuck running an online business that winds up being unable to generate you income either.

Creating a Business Plan, Setting goals and Budget

Whether you use someone's free of cost online business strategy, pay a higher priced professional for one or create it yourself, some kind of plan is a crucial tool for you, the business owner, to successfully expand your company as an online business. A clearly written <u>business plan</u> will go a long way in helping you narrow down your focus and sharpen your skills as a business person; you will be able to think ahead, plan, and double check everything to ensure you are on the right track. The significance of the internet is that it is a place where you can use the experience of practically hundreds of experts in a specific area of interest and bring the best techniques you learnt from them towards the success of your own goals. The internet has indeed become a source for tapping into the greatest of other individuals' previous experiences while expanding your knowledge at the same time. Besides assisting you set your initial plan such as identifying your goals, setting your monetary goals and evaluating your business capacity, the online business plan enables you to gain access to other internet-based sources that boost the high quality of your plan. Whatever kind of online business you are interested in, the internet is the study source of choice for an innovative thinking online business owner. What you ought to accomplish first is to discover the category your online business belongs to. This will help you individualize your business thinking along a specific requirement. You could find software applications that could help with your projections for capital, executive recap, analysis of break-even earnings, goal or eyesight statement, expenses, budget plan quotes, and much more. The software application enables you to edit and individualize your company plan based on your specifications. If you're not confident about developing a great strategy then you could constantly choose to get help online, scanning through the several forums and sites which may lead you to an expert who can be of help to you. If your spending plan is reduced, you can start with a really easy synopsis of your goals and aspirations which could help you along the way to refocus your thoughts and achieve your objectives. The success of every business plan depends on the set goals and objectives. It is also important to say that budgets are always influenced by the amount of money you have available for your online business. This could really affect the performance of the business especially at the start when it usually seems to be very difficult to break even.

However, you just need to think about those ideas you feel will help your business grow. Goals tell you where you want to go to and objectives tell you how you want to get there. It is also very important that you involve everyone that will help you towards actualizing your objectives when you are setting the plans for them. Ensure your goals are 'SMART' Specific, Measurable, Attainable, Relevant and Time-bound. You can check out Business Plans or Business Plans UK for sample ways to write your business plan or you can also sign up with the available packages on their website if you feel the need to do so.

Designing a well secured professional website

Every online business owner knows that a professional website boosts revenues. A website is a sign of your business and is a direct depiction of your organizational requirements. A poorly produced or messed up site will just cause visitors to look somewhere else online. Once released, your website becomes your company's image. It mirrors your values, items you offer, quality of services you provide, and your commitment to your customers. It is your most important method of featuring your online business. Designing a professional website that will market your services or products to your customers can take some time and effort, though the result will be increased revenues and customer satisfaction. The following describes basic factors involving in creating a professional website:

Register a Domain name: Deciding on an expert domain name is important to making sure visitors may locate your site. When selecting a domain name, consider your company approach and your services or products. Ensure your domain is simple to spell and remember .com is one of the most common ending for an organizational business URL and is additionally an ending that can be used when you want a global reach for your online business. By this I mean that, it is very important to know that if you want your business to be seen internationally, it is always much better registering your domain using .com unless if not available for your choice of domain name.

Register for web Hosting: Web Hosting enables you to save your web site on a hosting server that is accessible 24 hours a day / 7 days a week. Always make sure that you acquire an internet web hosting package deal that fulfills all your demands.

Design the website: You may either choose a professional to design the site, buy a web designing template, or you do it by yourself. Working with a professional to make your website will certainly indicate that your web site will certainly be of top quality. Acquiring an expert website design template could cause an item that does not complement your company image. Building your website by yourself can consume much of your time could be very discouraging unless you currently have the skills of an internet developer.

Show Customer Testimonials: By showing client reviews, you are revealing to prospective clients that you can be counted on, and your product and service is of high quality. Your clients will not provide you with their credit card details if they have doubts concerning the safety of your site. Make sure your website visitors are able to see that your site is secured with an SSL certificate when they are about to 'check out' products they have bought on your website.

Internet site Loading Time: The advised size of a website should be about 40-60 K. This size is recommended so that website visitors should not wait too long for the website to load. In many cases, if they need to stand by for longer than 20 seconds, they will move on to yet another website. To maintain a reasonable browsing time, always utilize minimal graphics on your website.

Keep Your Web site updated: To develop and sustain returning customers, you will need to provide your website visitors a reason a visit again and buy again from you in the future. To achieve this, you will need to update your website with new contents on a regular basis. New material may originate from such sources as news clips, articles, suggestions and so on. Your content should relate to your site and should consistently make your visitors want to come back another day. Unprofessionally created internet websites do not equate into revenues. When looking at your very own website, ask yourself this question; will I buy a product or service from the business? Your internet website is the most vital revenue generating tool you have. Your website visitor's first impression matters as that will instantly dictate whether or not you are going to make a revenue from the visit or not. Professionalism and trust are crucial elements of organizational success. Professionalism and reliability will certainly be seen in your website and business if everything is in order.

Structuring Your URLs For Search Engine Optimization: It could be frustrating to track all key areas you need to track in order to prepare your website for <u>search engine optimisation</u>. There are also many businesses that can help you do this. You could simplify the process of online <u>search engine optimization</u> simply by condensing the core components to these three factors: keywords, tags, and backlinks. Once you have a firm understanding of these key areas, there is another crucial area you need to keep an eye on and that is appealing to those that view your website in an online search engine result. Certainly, your usage of keywords as well as tags should be able to help you get discovered by customers in an online search engine result; particularly as you are most likely going to be using your primary keywords in the URL of your website. Another thing to recognize is that many web pages of your website are going to show up in search engines. These are web pages that are not merely your <u>primary domain</u>, name for example <u>http://www.thesecretcodetosucessandwealth.com/shop.html</u> and you will definitely want these links to appeal to your website visitors and the search engines too. The most effective method to use and accomplish this is to be sure that the part of the URL affixed to the end of your 'home page' consists of words, as opposed to number or such things like "page1," "webpage 2," etc. Hence, you will definitely provide those who see the link of your website a clearer understanding of what they will certainly view on the webpage while also making it less complicated for them to share your web page, and making it even more possible that they will certainly share the right anchor text when linking others to your webpage. Lastly, a URL using a correct, detailed anchor text added to the end will make it easier for search engines to crawl your webpage, and for them to collect the information they require to enable customers to find your online business. Together, you will definitely be able to complete the process by merely taking note of what the URL looks like on each page of your website.

Why you cannot afford to neglect data backup

Picture a scenario where you want to work on your computer, you turn it on to boot the computer and there is nothing to display. The data on your system is gone. You've merely dropped everything you have worked on for the last years. All your Adwords projects, websites, templates, Ebooks, Excel files all disappeared. Everything big and small just gone like that. Just how will you feel? How do you go about recovering your data and records? It is estimated that about 70% of businesses that go through data loss go out of business within 12 months. The reality is that many individuals never ever recuperate from losing all their records and data. To prevent this from happening to you, it is suggested that you backup your data without delay and more essentially on a regular basis. You can make use of a zip drive, a CDR/DVD writer, a USB drive or a safe online storage solution. Using any of the above is much better compared to not using anything at all and wanting the best. In US for example, data loss has made businesses to lose billions of dollars.

It is important that your information back up is done weekly. The best method to do this is to use an information backup system. Get 4 blank disks. Tag these disks Week 1, Week 2, Week 3 and Week 4. At the beginning of the month, make effort to download all your critical data and records on the Week 1 disk and repeat this procedure on Week 2, 3 and 4. When you carry out this type of measure on a regular basis, it will certainly help you to ensure that you have an updated back up of your data. Following this strategy will help you to ensure that regardless of what happens, your saved information will certainly never ever be more than 1 week old, and you will also have 3 other copies of your records stored away that are less than a month old. This is primarily straightforward and very efficient to do. Microsoft Windows has its very own backup software application features. Apple Mac users can make use of Apples Data backup software and iDisk backup service. You can start the process of backing up your data today. It is essential that you begin now to prevent unnecessary information or data loss. 76% of data loss comes as result of human error and hardware failures. When you maintain a good data backup strategy, the cost of recovering from the loss could drastically be reduced in the long run. You have taken very important step to build your online business. Therefore, more needs to be done by you to ensure you protect your data from loss by taking the appropriate action.

Virtual Dedicated Server Hosting is the hottest level in SEO marketing as online business owners acquire the very best solutions that are dedicated to them without paying a fortune for that. The outcomes are mind blowing with multifold benefits and significant customer connections for their cash converting websites. High quality and efficiency combined with cost is the essential aspect of <u>Virtual Private Server(VPS) hosting</u>, which every seasoned provider should handle. Many online businesses have their website hosted over a shared server that runs efficiently for their business. However if the internet traffic to your website suddenly increased with many visitors, this could mean that your online business website and the hosting server could be at the verge of slowing down. That's why many high performing businesses opt in for <u>VPS Hosting</u> to maximize their business potentials and generate more sales. However, for some businesses that are just starting out, it could be costly when your company is small and needs fewer resources in a secured and stable environment. Online Virtual Web servers are the only possible alternative that you may upgrade to, in order to manage this situation and protect your company. Migrating your websites to a reliable <u>VPS hosting provider</u> could reward your online business in the long run based on the effort you have put in.

Integrating Payment Processing System

<u>Electronic payment processing system</u> adds to a client's satisfaction. These methods of payment have made all kinds of online business transactions possible with the click of a mouse. Electronic payment processing system can help towards reducing your Company's operational cost and expenses. At the same time, using digital payment system can easily help your online business to boost customer loyalty and sales. A great number of service providers offer

solutions to payment processing transactions using electronic invoices, credit card purchases and many other methods. This additionally removes the challenges of using manual payment processing system and reducing the handling time and enhancing the accuracy of processing payments. The options allow the customers and end users to appreciate the systems set up while offering countless ways to engage more with the service provider.

The advantages of the <u>electronic payment system</u> delivered by prominent service providers include:

- ♦ Enhanced presence of processes, that feature invoice and payment procedures
- ♦ Considerable reduction in your online business expenses
- ♦ Enhanced savings
- ♦ Increase in cash flow
- ♦ Improved customer satisfaction and loyalty.

Considerably enhanced ability to deal with changes in the dynamic company atmosphere.

Ability to take care of some exceptions, freeing up resources leading to allocation of more time on other goals you need to accomplish in your online business. All these possibilities joined with the cutting edge <u>online payment processing system</u> adds to your competitive edge. It further helps you in achieving increased cash flow in your online business.

Optimizing for search engines to find your business

Online Business is a very important business model. You have to equip yourself with the right tools and resources needed to help your business succeed. Every day, an increasing number of businesses are working very hard to ensure that their websites are high up in ranking to enhance their performance and maximize profits. Therefore it is very essential that your online business does not fall short of this expectation if your intention is to make more sales and increase cash flow. Online search engine Optimization or SEO is a term commonly used today by many e-commerce websites. For the past couple of years and many years to come, online search engine will become one of the best online tools for customers to find the websites that they want to visit or the product or info they require. Most people that use the search engines like Google, yahoo or Bing usually focus on just the top 10 search results in the very first web page. Making it to the first web page and possibly to the top 3 is a good way to check websites that have been very well optimized organically on the search engine. You website will certainly acquire a higher possibility of being clicked on when you are placed higher on the search engine. More traffic to your website will likely convert into earnings. It is necessary to get your website to the top page using advertising or make your ranking to get you to the top page organically. On a daily basis, each website owner has the opportunity to make their website ranking much higher by making use of the online search engine optimization. If you get a hundred visitors or more on a daily basis, you could make good sales everyday if they convert. If you acquire just twenty to fifty hits a day, you could just make one or two sales if not any at all. There are several aspects of your website that you will need to change to maximize your ranking in the search engine. This will certainly involve finding the target keywords used in searching for a specific product in your niche. You might also have to rewrite your website content to ensure you have the correct keywords on your website without making it too complicated. There are certain guidelines and standards to abide by when making your website's content suitable and favorable for search engine optimization. You will certainly need to work together with other website owners to ensure you can get backlinks from them to your website. The additional inbound and outbound links you could get will lead to web traffic which is one of the components that search engines use to rank websites.

Advertising and Promoting your Business Website

As an online entrepreneur, you might wish to review the marketing methods that you are using if you are really marketing your business accordingly. When it involves marketing an online business, you will certainly find that it is less complicated to market an online business than it is to market an office based business. There are various strategies you can use to market your business online. Among the numerous methods that you could use when marketing your business online is using an online forum. Online forums are networks where internet marketers and other individuals are able to come together and discuss activities or interests they want to share or talk about. There are many Online forums that allow participating members to have just what is referred to as a signature. You could add your signature at the end of each post you want to post on the forums you belong to so that it will always show up at the end of your posts. It is not uncommon for an online forum moderator to permit signatures to consist of business hyperlinks, like a link to your online outlet or online website. When you use internet message boards or online forums, more exposure to your online business is generated. Yet another way that you may market your small online business is by joining a pay per click advertising program, like Google Adwords. By your company joining a popular pay per click marketing program, you are less likely to experience troubles linked with harmful clicks as the Google Adwords campaign is meticulously supervised, to make sure that you do not end up wasting money on advertising and marketing for your small business. A link exchange is when one website owner, like you, agrees to exchange your website link or banner with another website owner, free of charge, as long as they return the favor. If you are looking for free or low-priced methods for marketing your online business, a link exchange might be the perfect alternative for you. When it pertains to operating an online business, web searches may additionally play a key role in the web traffic that you and your website could receive. That is why it is vital that your website, whether it is used for offering items or services, is maximized for the online search engine ranking. This procedure is typically described as online search engine optimization. When it concerns <u>search engine optimization</u>, your website content is vital. Your website should be filled up with content that the online search engine will be able to index, along with contents that your website visitors may review. If you need help with this, you might wish to think of working with a <u>Search Engine Optimization specialist</u> or an expert content writer. The above mentioned advertising strategies are simply a few of the many ways that you could utilize to help enhance your online business revenue. It is even better if you could do more to improve your chances of success.

Chapter 2
Integrating Social Media and Networking In Your Online Business

<u>In This Chapter</u>

YouTube and Video Marketing Strategies

Beyond Visible Social Media Buttons

Use of WordPress for Online Business

Collaborating Across Sites

Use of Viral Marketing

Paying Attention to Terms and Conditions of Use

Press Release Marketing

Advanced Backlink Strategies

Use of Social Media Insights

Why Integrating Social Media is so Important

The Benefits of Social Media for Your Online Business

YouTube and Video Marketing Strategies

If you are currently rated first in your keyword, and you are making for instance $200/day from that keyword, how do you enhance it to $250 or $300 if you are currently rated? When you have the presumption that your website is already maximized and has an excellent sales rate, then the next thing you have to do is increase the quantity of web traffic to your site. For instance if your one hundred visitors per day is making your $200/day, increasing the site visitors to 300/day will certainly make you $300/day. When improving web traffic to your website, you have to keep in mind that the website traffic that you send out to your website needs to be targeted. Sending 6000 website visitors who are not interested in buying the product you are selling will not generate any revenue for you. The most targeted individuals are those who are seeking the item itself. For instance people that are targeting" Apple iPhone 5 Reviews," (Apple iPhone 5 being the product). Anyone that is targeting this keyword is most likely ready to buy the phone. Another targeted keyword technique that you can use is to target the problem. An example would be people who are searching for keywords such as "how do I find a date," or "how do I repair my Computer". Before we carry on, it is important to explain that the examples discussed here are mostly used for websites that are currently generating revenues for you, and you intend to generate more revenue from this specific website. If your website does not have an excellent sales conversion orgood customer satisfaction, it will be better for you to implement previous steps like search engine optimization, keyword targeting, backlinking etc to maximize the web traffic to your website.

So let's now talk about the strategy. If, for example, you joined "weight loss" as a specific niche and you target the keywords "how to lose weight." First thing you need to do is to type that keyword into YouTube. You will then see a list of videos. You now go on to click on a video clip that has higher number of views. For example, I decide on the very first video" 7 simple steps to instant weight loss" as it has a very higher number of views on YouTube. You will just need to click on the statistics button. You will then see a graph that shows the total views this video clip has acquired over time from the moment the video clip was uploaded till the current date. You have to locate a video with a graph which is constantly receiving views. A flat graph implies that the video no longer obtains any type of additional website traffic and is of no use to you. Once you have found a suitable video, go ahead and click the YouTube video button. This will show you the description of the video clip, the Category of the video clip and very importantly the video tags. The Tags on YouTube videos help videos to get indexed by search engine so that they could be found when someone searches for the video or similar. YouTube classifies their videos using the tags, and for instance where this specific video was found, you will see other video clips which are similar to this video "7 simple steps to instant weight loss" video clip. It is very crucial to remember that if someone views a YouTube video clip, the next thing that a website visitor will do at the end of watching that video is to click on a related video. I am sure that if you use YouTube that you will certainly do the same. Now remember that this particular video clip could have over 10 thousand views. Picture your video turning up as an associated video clip to this "7 simple steps to instant weight loss." Well, YouTube Tags could land you a place as a relevant video clip. So indeed, it's incredibly easy. All you have to do is make a video clip (try to make the video clip as a top quality video if not much better compared to the existing video clip) and replicate the tags.

Beyond Visible Social Media Buttons

Online business owners are striving to discover methods to boost social media sharing of their websites. There are some methods that could be used to do this and among one of the most noticeable ways is to make it straightforward for readers to do so. Website visitors would not wish to invest half an hour of their time searching for a share button on your online business website. It is very important that you make the share buttons visible on your website so that visitors can find them easily. One advantage of sharing your content is that it creates backlinks to your website. Google ranks your website based on the number of backlinks that you have as they consider your website to be an important website when you have many backlinks linking to your website. Google will certainly prioritize your website, and you will surely end up with additional traffic compared to other websites. At some point, you will produce a social buzz and your ranking will certainly enhance the performance of your online business. It is also very important to consider the option of using the word of the mouth in your advertising and marketing. You need to take care not to have too many share buttons on your website as this simply puzzles readers. Website visitors do not always have the time to share your content on the internet and they might even choose not to share anything. You could use few share buttons on your website and most importantly sticking to the most popular share buttons like Facebook like, Facebook share, Twitter, LinkedIn, Pinterest, Email, Google $\pm$, etc. Do not be shy to ask individuals or friends to share your website. At the bottom of each blog ask them to provide their views on your blog post and to share your article. Make sure that the share buttons are properly configured. Twitter is a great example of a website that only approves 140 characters and blog site titles with more than this number of characters will certainly not be shared on Twitter unless the title is edited. There is nothing worse than checking out an amazing write-up to discover that you cannot find the buttons to share the content. Your website visitors will certainly become disillusioned to find out that they have wasted most of their time attempting to find the share buttons. It is definitely a good idea that you add the share buttons at the end of each post. By doing this, your readers may not skip the possibility of sharing your website with others. One more option is to have the share buttons behind the article as they cannot be missed out on there.

Use of WordPress for Online Business

With the existing progression in modern technology, the internet has become one of the greatest places to set up and advertise a small company. WordPress comes with some advantages which include:

Free Open Source: Unlike many other open source programs which are completely free of charge and yet have hidden objectives behind them, WordPress for websites and blogs is completely free. With WordPress comes unlimitedly usage though you might have to pay for some plugins and you may have to subscribe to WordPress hosting based on your need. This is one of the best attributes you can obtain from WordPress.org services. It is always better to go for wordpress.org which comes free when you buy a domain name as more secured.

Secured Safety: Making use of WordPress assures you of making profits by providing security to your website. The

safety of WordPress permits you to trust the use of WordPress developer software to protect your website from malicious competitors.

Plugins for More Performance: The WordPress plugins allows you to include even more image galleries that will look appealing to your website. WordPress has many plugins that the website user can easily locate and use by integrating them.

Easy Blogging: As a blogging website, WordPress has become vast in blogging activities. WordPress developers have produced a simple method of attaching a blog site to your internet website. This boosts your visibility online as many website visitors can easily visit your website and see what your business is offering them. In addition, WordPress developed an easy way of categorizing and tagging to make the internet experience even more pleasant and fun. Other additional options such as spam guard and security features to defend your website from having mundane attacks like hacking have also been developed. With this and other options, your website rank on significant search engine optimization might boost considerably. Having more targeted visitors is a potential that your revenues could rise. Your website visitor can easily select many alternatives readily available from the WordPress website plugins as required. For instance, a visitor might choose to connect to a blog site rather than the whole internet site. WordPress is a great content management system with different plugins that bring fantastic performance to the system. Nonetheless, it is suggested that the use of the most crucial WordPress plugins on your website has great advantages though the use of excessive plugins can drastically reduce your website/blog loading time. You are therefore required to identify the most essential WordPress plugins so that these are put on your WordPress blog.

Collaborating Across sites

For Off-Page Optimization, you will have to work together with other websites that have comparable interests to negotiate link exchanges. Online search engines place the popularity of a site by the many inbound links to the website. These links may be created using different methods such as:

Posting Access on Blogs: Doing this will secure you a hyperlink back to your site, and if you make use of one of your keywords, it will certainly count for your website. You definitely need to start blogging about your business or anything of interest soon.

Create Write-ups Concerning Your Target Market: As an expert in your niche, you will have a great deal of topics to talk about and share with others as many people are anxiously waiting to read just what you have to say especially if it is a rich, informative content. You can add hyperlinks to your article, and if another person uses your article on their website, then you have an added link. Make use of Internet 2.0 or Social Media websites: YouTube, MySpace, Facebook, LinkedIn and Twitter are just examples of the websites you could use to create backlinks to your website. Remember that, these websites are for networking with both like minded people and others and you will need to join networks or groups where you can find the right people you are looking for. Search Engine Optimization will certainly do more for your online business than you could imagine. You might choose to optimize your website by yourself if you know how to do it, provided you can take time on a regular basis to monitor your progression, and apply new techniques, or you might outsource it to an SEO expert that understands what can be done.

Use of Viral Marketing

Viral Marketing is a great marketing tool that is very powerful enough to help you generate more traffic to your online business website. When you consider how a virus spreads from one person to another, you will agree with me that many people can easily be infected by a virus merely by contact with someone already infected thereby transferring the virus to a greater number of people. When individuals who get infected by the virus share it with other people, it eventually reaches a point where all of them become ill as a result of the virus and hence the virus goes pandemic. It is exactly the same mode of operation with the idea of viral marketing. It is an intention to get the idea out to everybody to spread the marketing message around faster and quicker with the intention of reaching many people. Now, can I start by asking you if you have ever considered the use of an E-book for your viral advertising campaign? You create an E-book ... a really great one that has links to your internet websites, to your products and services, blogs and other solutions you want to offer to others. You can share it with three or more people. You can share it on your social media networks. In essence, you have to encourage those you shared it with to offer it to their friends, family members and networks. Just like a wild fire, the e-book could spread across the internet reaching many people than you can imagine. Digital information reproduces effortlessly and in a very fast technique and so before you realize it, many individuals could be reading your free of charge E-book. Make sure that you let those individuals know that they have the authority to share the E-book around the internet. When you create the E-book, you can give people specific rights. One of those rights could be permission to provide guidance to all other people. You may write the E-book on your own, use private label material or you could choose a ghostwriter to prepare the ebook for you. There are a number of methods you can use to produce an E-book. Once you have your E-book draft ready, make use of software application to develop your E-book.

The Many Facets of Viral Advertising: Initially, email was the only way that viral advertising and marketing was begun. However, viral advertising has gone from just being an email advertising method to being advanced in many other ways even through avenues like YouTube and social media. There are different strategies you can use towards accomplishing the goal of developing a successful viral advertising and marketing project. Seven of those strategies are:

Email: The use of email is nevertheless a little bit of more challenging to use as an increasing number of government regulations are put on it. Still ... it does the job. E-newsletters: This is an expansion of email as it is a very effective tool. If you enjoy offering highly valued updates to your clients, a newsletter will go further towards providing an opportunity to network and share interests with your clients as well as many other potential clients that might subscribe to your updates.

Blogging: The use of essential tools on your online business website with the intention of making it possible for bloggers to connect with one another is an excellent way to inform people about your services and products. Blog writers have their perception which they share about brand-new services and products.

Chat room: A live discussion of your internet site can and does encourage interaction among your clients. To find out more about the needs of your clients, you could communicate with them using the chat room.

Tell-a-friend Button: If you include this with a declaration saying that e-mail addresses provided will never be shared with third parties, you may enhance your client's list significantly.

Video Clips: Including amazing video clips on your web site will certainly increase your website traffic as visitors will love to watch what you have on the video.

Flash Games: it could be slightly expensive to start with. However, they are very efficient tools to use and get your viral marketing project out there to the general public. When they are introduced, they call for absolutely nothing more from you.

Using Google Analytics

For several companies, moving into the E-commerce industry may be a challenging procedure. Not only is the website design vital, but you will also need to make sure that you are getting your website seen by optimizing it appropriately. This could be an incredibly tricky procedure and it could be extremely challenging to identify exactly how potential clients are taking to your website and where problematic areas are. Google Analytics is a free online application that offers a very wide range of tools that will help you generate a variety of information regarding your website visitors. A wide range of tools will be made available to you once you have created a Google Analytics account. Most of the beneficial tools are readily available in the dashboard panel where you can observe the usage trends of your site. It consists of graphs presenting all vital information about your daily website usage. Those charts will enable you to measure total and average number of visits, webpage views, and average time the visitors spent on the site. It also enables you to check the bounce rate, and the percentage of website visits from new visitors. You could map specifically where your website visits are coming from. You may also determine which among your web pages are receiving the most number of views. By means of these useful features, you will easily determine what exactly is noticeable or undesirable on your website. You will also be able to check your site demographics. All of these make up the basic facets of Analytics. You could familiarize yourself with some specific aspects of Analytics to make sure that it does not supply less important opinion like alerts. Alerts enable you to be updated on the new aspects of your website like advertising campaigns. Google Analytics will then supply all necessary feedback once it reaches your set goal. Goals are an exceptionally helpful attributes as they enable you to establish funnels to track exactly how users are browsing through the vital locations of your website for example from the shopping cart to the check out and completion of the shopping. For any type of E-commerce website, the primary aim is to obtain as many visitors or users as possible. Payment portals or gateways play a very important role in getting online sales, so you need to get a reliable service provider. You can easily determine the most

viewed web pages of your website by creating sets of funnels. This feature is extremely beneficial especially if you want to boost your online sales without engaging in too much trial and error. Google Analytics have other features that you need to check out if you want to improve the performance of your website.

Paying Attention to Terms and Conditions of Use

The terms and conditions of E-commerce sites are regulated and controlled under the E-commerce Regulation 2002. To point out, it is the companies' duty to provide the right company terms and conditions to their clients. By doing this, you can ensure the growth and success of your business. It will also minimize your liability. The terms and conditions will serve as a legal contract between you and your customer. It will also help your clients determine how you regulate your business. Your clients definitely need to read your terms and conditions before buying any of your products.

E-commerce rules can be applied to any of the following:

Companies that sell products or services online, by e-mail, or through SMS

Companies that advertise online, by e-mail, or through SMS

Companies that store or transfer electronic content for their clients

Companies that provide access to communication networks

Writing Your Terms and Conditions: We all live in the business age that requires written agreements. However, online businesses have their own way of dealing with clients. As an online business owner, you can communicate with your customers through your website's terms and conditions. Your terms and conditions will ensure the growth and success of your business only if they are properly and comprehensively written. You need to provide all necessary information like the cost of the product, delivery or shipping fees, liability limitations, methods of payment, jurisdiction, and offer durations. The terms of your website should provide a clearer picture to your customers thus helping them to make the right decision in buying your products.

Legally Binding Contract: As it can be considered as a legally binding contract, this document will be enforceable every time your customer clicks on the box labeled "I agree and accept the terms and conditions." Always keep in mind that this powerful document does not have any drawbacks.

Your Obligation: It is always your obligation to manage your business according to your terms and conditions. You should never charge any fees that are not mentioned or disclosed in your binding contract. Your customers will only follow the contracts that are made between them and you (the business owner). Always keep in mind that your customers can always sue you for breach of agreement.

Jurisdiction Matter: The jurisdiction matter refers to the law where the service provider is subject to where he or she is based rather than where his or her customers are based.

Privacy Policy: You only need to have a privacy policy if you collect personal information from your clients or use cookies and other types of tracking technologies. The main components of the documents should incorporate for example the essence of the whole contract, when it has been made, offer and acceptance, information updates on the website, customer account and confidentiality. It should also contain information about the price, VAT, payments, delivery information, and risks that might be involved.

Return of Goods: reasons and procedure, disclaimer, limitations of seller's liability, Intellectual property protection. It should also contain a comprehensive "User Policy", User Safety information, prohibitions against customer offenses, legal provisions such as Warranties, Indemnities, Exclusions, other important legal provisions etc.

Press Release Marketing

If you want to boost the performance of your business, creating press releases would help you a lot. Other people might think that it is just a marketing strategy, but you should never ignore its importance. Press releases will give you the chance to promote or advertise your business without making it seem that you are attempting to sell your products to your readers. You will surely reach many potential readers if you write your press releases correctly. When writing a press release, you need to write in third person all the time. It should sound like it is news rather than a promotional content. It is like you are writing news to announce your business without mentioning that you are the actual owner of the business. Of course, you need to present each and everything positively. You have no limits when it comes to writing a press release, so you should always keep in mind that even little things count. You may include hiring information in your company or the new products that you are about to launch soon. There are tools that can help you in writing a powerful press release in just a few minutes.

Advanced Backlink Strategies

One of the most important things that will contribute to your website's success is backlink building. You can do this by creating links on different relevant websites that will point back to your own website. This will also help you in boosting your website's traffic and search engine rankings. This might be time-consuming, but I assure you that it will contribute a lot to the success of your online business. You can make high quality backlinks by providing high quality content to your readers. If your readers think that your content is beneficial, they will never think twice in sharing it to their friends. This way, you will create organic backlinks. Apart from providing high quality content to your website, you can also increase the chances of getting more readers and generating more online sales by putting social media widgets on your site. By doing this, your readers will find it easier to share your content. They will be able to share your website's content in just a click of the mouse. You may put social media widgets that will allow your readers to share your contents on Facebook, Twitter, Google Plus, Digg, and other social media sites. You may also build backlinks by doing link exchange. You may build partnerships with reputable websites and ask their permission to post your website link on their sites. You may also post their website links on your site in exchange. Another powerful way of creating backlinks is by writing articles and submitting them to article directories. You do not need to spend hours in creating unique and high quality content because there are tools that will help you minimize your writing efforts. Just check out some of the links on chapter 7 to sign up for instant access to the Article Spinning tool and Article Submission tool. In some cases, you might have to pay for the tool but it is worth it.

Use Of Social Media Insights

Maximize Success: Most companies use social media because it can help them connect to their target market easily. It is always affordable to use social media in advertising. However, you need to understand that social media marketing, just like any other type of marketing, requires thorough planning.

Tap Customer Needs and Wants: Social media marketing is indeed one of the easiest ways to determine the insights of your customers about your products and services. Your company and products will surely trend on social media sites if your customers are really impressed with them. Starbucks is one of the companies that do social media marketing really well. They engage with their customers by creating a social media page that provides information about their company and products. Starbucks is indeed one of the richest companies out there and that is why its social media managers can afford to pay the market research firms to collect and present important data on their behalf. Powerful social media marketing can take months so you need much patience.

Why Integrating Social Media is so Important

Social media can always be beneficial for both small and medium-sized companies. Social media monitoring focuses on every specific aspect of a business without applying manipulations. It also has many filtering options that you can choose from. Here are the most powerful benefits of social media monitoring to your online business or any small and medium-sized company:

The suggestions and comments of your customers will help in the growth and development of your company.

Quick responses will provide you with better position in the market.

It helps you in determining the latest trends in the industry as well as the ways on how to engage with your current and potential customers.

It will give you a platform that will help you in featuring your products and services.

It will help you in encouraging all of your satisfied clients in sharing their positive reviews on your products.

It will help you in tracking your social media growth.

It will help you in evaluating the performance of your competitors

It will help you in determining the top sources and users in the industry

It will help you in tracking the right keywords that will help you in boosting your customer base.

Here are the ways on how to start integrating social media monitoring in your search strategy: Using the right social media tools.

Analyzing social keywords and tags – this involves applying social media tagging and social bookmarking.

Gaining customer insights – this involves listening to the concerns of your potential customers and addressing them. Having a better focus – this will involve the integration of Google Analytics to collect information and improve the search ranking strategies of your website.

The Advantages of Social Media in Your Business

Social media has many advantages for business owners like you. First, it will help you in building a huge online client and audience base. It is easier to find potential clients online because people who have the same interests always connect with each other. It is not just powerful but also affordable. You do not need to spend much money just to connect with your potential buyers. However, social media advertising may cost you some money. Social media marketing is indeed one of the strategies that you need to consider when it comes to boosting your website's search engine rankings.

Chapter 3
Attracting Customers and Keeping Them

In This Chapter

Having Knowledge of What People are Looking for.

Why You Need A Business Mentor

Building Loyal Customers by Focusing on Relationships

Use of Webinar for Your Online Business

Advertising Effectively Using Demographics & Psychographics

Outsourcing to Leverage Your Time

Hiring a Virtual Assistant

Finding Unique Ways to Delight Your Customers

Having Competitive Prices on Your Products

Showcasing Customer Reviews

The Power of Spiritual, Emotional, Mental & Physical Well Being on Your Business

Recognizing Business Risks and Understanding How to Deal With Them

Reaching Out to Potential Partners

Having Knowledge of What People are Looking for

One big deal in setting up an online business is building a persuasive website. This will eventually serve as your window to the world and its appearance will inevitably convey your business potential and capabilities without the need of putting up an establishment in an actual business location. Since website needs server, you have the option of using a general hosting or the Virtual Private Server (VPS) wherein you will not have to abide to any rules and regulations. In addition, improvement of website and doing minor or major alterations are possible even if you don't have much knowledge about coding and the likes. You can make the site appealing with the use of simple platforms and other techniques.

Whenever people look for information through the web, a huge number of recommended sources can be viewed in the search engine results. So if you want your online business to be visible to the online viewers, you should have a clear understanding of how the internet works.

To boost its ranking or visibility, you can invest and ask assistance from experts in Search Engine Optimization (SEO). Take note that the search engine or website has algorithms to follow and certainly, these experts know the ins and outs that may include keywords search and proper writing of the content. Designing a website is crucial to creating a remarkable image of your online business to your potential consumers. Although there can be a huge number of pages that focus on various topics, products or services, you have to take note that it should be natural in progress. For instance, in the home page section, you should provide a description of what your business is all about. Along with its persuasive writing, it would be best to provide links that would allow your visitors to obtain information about you and your business.

A section about the Frequently Asked Questions (FAQ) and links should be added to your website. This is because not all visitors will read the entire page or content of your website but rather, they will look for answers that concern them. In this manner, the term "surfing" comes in the picture.

If you do want your business to succeed, focusing on social media is paramount. In this medium, blogging has also become an important strategy which online businesses have been using to be closer to their prospective consumers since it can channel information and daily updates about the business, products and services. It only makes sense that you should include this within your website. However, it is of utmost importance that you should be consistent with blog postings.

Undeniably, there are a number of false or fraudulent systems all over the internet. With this in mind, before people make any business transaction with you, they will be looking for reliable and concrete information. In your online business, you need to add business contact details with its physical business address, images of staff and owner in your website. This will bring human touch that can build trust, thereby making it easier to persuade your potential consumers.

After setting up your business website, keeping and maintaining it on a regular basis should be highly considered. There is a number of accessible software that will allow you to monitor and analyze the movements of your visitors. Furthermore, Google analytics is free and it will enable you to excel in your field by setting up goals and targets.

Using Keywords to Trigger Sales: Working and earning money at home is now a common thing to do. You become your own boss when you start an online business or work from home business. However, only few people find success at this kind of work, because most of the people fail to understand the big picture of how vital search engine optimization is. In making money as a search engine marketer (SEM), it is a crucial thing to understand that you solely focus on keywords when you create content for your website. More so, you need to know which keywords you should pay attention to.

There are the three types of reasons why people use the internet:

Academic research

Product research

Product purchase

When you look at these three types of searches, you can easily guess which one can bring you money (the one with the word purchase). However, most people fail to see this, and as time progresses they end up with keywords that bring them very little income.

In addition, using "product research" keyword is not a complete waste of time because this can help get shoppers before they make their purchase. However, should you opt to tackle on both sides, make sure that you first make good use of the keyword – "product purchase."

Furthermore, build your site using "product purchase" keywords and target keywords such as "Best prices iPhone 5 mobile phone" instead of targeting keywords that researchers will commonly use such as "iPhone price comparisons" or "different types of iPhones."

Moreover, gradually start to include "product research" keywords, and this is a good opportunity to create backlinks leading to more "profitable" contents.

In online business, search engine optimization is a multilayered problem that you must understand. If you want to achieve real success, then you have to understand all aspects of SEO. Now that you know and understand the different keyword searches, you are certainly an inch closer to understanding how Search Engine Marketing (SEM) can help you make money.

Why You Need a Business Mentor

Many people find it difficult to start online business especially if it is their first time to venture into it. However, it could be made simpler if you have a business mentor that will guide you through this transition. Now, let us explore the fears that people express when they want to venture into online business or even if they are already doing it.

Fear of Failing: What if we want to expand, and yet no one likes what we want to achieve? What if current customers leave us just because of a move they didn't approve of for some reason? These are some of the questions that some online business companies face especially when generating low income. So, you are not alone. Think of the purpose or reason why you wanted to start the online business. You will surely find inspiration by doing so. Moreover, if you know that your product and services are the best quality, then you have that obligation to spread the information about your services to the society at large. You have that gift and opportunity to help others who are searching for one solution or another. However, if you choose not to, then the company's growth is at stake. Moreover, [this would be] a waste of potential that the community could have loved.

Fear of Succeeding: If your company received a thousand orders or more in just a day than the previous month or year, will it put you out of place just because you can't handle the load? Will you be labeled as a poor customer service provider just because it took you longer to deliver the products than the agreed schedule?

This could happen to you. Receiving a thousand orders for your products wouldn't hurt you if all the products you are selling are automated. Moreover, will you still wait for that wake-up call? Would you wait for orders to pour in before you get the right number of staff? What is more difficult is that you are the main person to post all the products to your customers. This will affect any of the plans that you have for your business because you can only focus on one thing and that is completing the orders. In addition, because of this experience, you can now see the vision for your business and how you can achieve it. Moreover, you'll see how important your business will be and that your products and services are crucial for you to succeed. Now, you and your team can spend three months planning how best to maximize your opportunities and grow your company.

You can also spend time planning on launching some new services. Moreover, you need to get in touch with your customers through use of customer relations management system, search engine campaigns, newsletter, blogs etc because in the long run it will really help you out.

Furthermore, getting that unexpected growth can be scary. However, it can be your wake-up call and a welcoming vision of what direction your business is going and what it needs to do to be stable.

Fear of What to Do Next: Are you inspired to expand your business and serve a larger part of the society? Are you already there but unaware?

What to Do and How You Will Support its Growth? What I can suggest would be, "Goal setting", yes goals are important, but what you must do is to make a very specific list of goals for the next month or two of your business. Now, do ask yourself what could happen to your business if you have to handle 200% of its growth this year alone? Must you hire someone? Do you need a better client management system? Do you have to outsource some of your work? You must be ready to look deeper to understand the secrets to online business growth. Moreover, this is also why you need a business mentor to guide you throughout this transition. That's why we are here for you.

Building Loyal Customers by Focusing on Relationships

The internet is not only limited to the opportunities that could be generated in the world of online business. It goes beyond the financial aspect since it allows people to build relationships even if they are miles away. Businesses and people can collaborate regardless of time and location.

Furthermore, online success gives opportunity for other businesses to team up with others.

The following are key points to remember if you are to merge with other online businesses to achieve online success and expansion.

Tap into the Goldmine of Affiliate Marketing: Affiliate marketing has many good things to offer. It makes sales much easier since it offers great opportunities from prominent websites and companies. These may include (a) selling products on your website and collecting commission when you close a deal or make successful sales and (b) if your business has products to sell, you can use other people's website to make profit.

Create a Joint Venture with a Fellow Business or Company: Promotion of products is made easier and practical with the joint forces of two online businesses. In this aspect, it allows them to feature one another's products using their own website. For instance: Business A has regular visitors of 20,000 monthly while Business B has the same for each month. When both of you see that there is no competition from each other, you could decide to share links or banners from each other on your websites to acquire more business exposure.

Team Up With the Customers You Already Have: Your consumers can be your best advertisers for your business. When you know how to team up with them, you are likely to provide your business a great boost. With this, give them incentives whenever they spread the word about your business and its products. In addition, you can build and establish relationship with them through social media sites such as YouTube, Facebook, Twitter, LinkedIn and more.

Use of Webinar for Your Online Business

Improving your business profile is one of the best ways to boost the success of your online business. This is made possible by conducting Webinar or Webinar series online as it will make a profound impression to a wider audience. However, there are still many individuals who are caught up in a puzzle on how they will exactly do it and make it a total achievement.

Moneymaking Webinar, as an example of a theoretical Webinar, could be the best answer in such a situation. Conducting a webinar has guidelines to follow to meet the demands and take control over the result you want to achieve. When managing a moneymaking

Webinar, take note of the five main things or questions as these will serve as your principles.

These May Include the Following:

What others will get out of the Webinar: This question is worth asking before launching any Webinar on any niche. If you fail to answer such question, then it is most likely, your audience will not be able to answer the same question at the end of the Webinar, making it worthless for them to attend another time. Therefore, focus and prepare on this before the launch and think about what your audience will get from the event.

What You Will Get Out of It: If you are going to conduct a Webinar with your time and effort, think ahead on what you can get in return although there are some who simply end up running this event without considering what they will get out of it at the end. For instance, if you are to conduct a moneymaking Webinar, returns are less expected unless you take one of these two actions (a) feature a product or (b) charge people to attend the event.

How People Will Attend: The internet allows you to reach a huge number of audiences at a time. With this in mind, there will be no problem about inability to attend in person, travel cost or delays. When delivering seminar in an auditorium, there is the potential that the venue could only be half-full and your audience could be feeling drowsy while the virtual room can also be the same. However, this will be less embarrassing unlike in the auditorium setup.

Nevertheless, you can take advantage of conducting a seminar online by promoting the program ahead of time and building audience before the scheduled time and date.

Know Your Way Around Your Presentation: Before you go live and conduct the Webinar, practice and learn every aspect of your presentation. You should have mastery over it and even though there is no need to face your audience personally, it is still a requirement that you as the presenter should be comfortable and confident. These are key factors that will make you a convincing and persuasive presenter. If you comply with these, then expect a positive and promising result.

Know Your Way Around Peripheral Topics: As part of the Webinar, there is the question and answer portion at the end. Your audience will throw diverse questions and some of these will not be likely related to your presentation. It would be shameful if you do not know how to respond to it and worst, do not know the answer. Nevertheless, you have to delve in and cover peripheral topics as this will help you answer and convey your response with confidence.

Advertising Effectively Using Demographics & Psychographics

Market research is fundamental to any kind of online business. Therefore, it is of utmost importance that you understand the two different terms which are demographics and psychographics.

Demographics: It simply refers to the common characteristics of your target market or people who are available to buy your products or services. Other areas considered include their annual income, type of occupation, age, region and the number of family members. It can also extend to the age of the children, the average value of their home, home ownership status and its locality i.e. whether rural or urban.

Psychographics: Unlike demographics that are easy to categorize, the psychographics are not. It goes beyond the characteristics of your targeted consumers. Psychographics cover the customer's lifestyles, psychology and behavior when it comes to buying things. It also considers several factors such as destination that customers like to travel to, their interests, different kinds of hobbies and their opinions.

To make it simple, the demographics relate to things that can be observed from the outside about the individuals who buy your products or services while psychographics understand the overall internal attributes and the behavior of buying.

You can obtain the necessary psychographics and demographics information of your targeted market through research. When you want to gain more details about demographic profile, you can make use of both the primary and secondary research. As for the psychographics, it will be done with the primary research. Therefore, a survey can be conducted with your targeted consumers. If you already have an online business, you can create a survey to know who already bought products or services from you.

When considering the advantages of getting the necessary information, it will be able to help you market and advertise your products or services effectively. It will give you a hint on what social media platform is best to use when trying to persuade your target market.

Furthermore, it will also broaden your understanding of their behavior such as "the thing" that makes them respond, the manner they answer to your marketing strategies and the motivation behind the purchase.

When you have a profound understanding of your target audience demographics and psychographics, you will be able to reap the fruits later on. Before that, you have to firstly conduct a survey and you can get them engaged with completing the survey by giving them opportunities to win a myriad of gadgets such as mobile phones, cameras etc. Another strategy you can use is offering your potential customers incentives such as gifts, vouchers and other enticing offers.

In advertising, there are many things to consider. When you intend to look for websites to work with, always look for websites that generate hundreds of thousand sales and have a minimum of 500,000 to 1 million unique impressions monthly. When this is done, you can go ahead and spread the word about your online business. This can be accomplished by use of selection of banners, establishing campaign objectives and duration of campaign. In organizing your plan, you have to determine the frequency and days your visitors can see the advertisement.

To make it more effective, specify the countries where your ads can be viewed.

As for the best placement of your website and the targeted ads, it has to be balanced. Therefore, you can start in between the available choices. For beginners, two days is a good start. If you are asked to mention the websites that you do not like to advertise, you can specify what you would prefer for example social networking sites, web portals, video centric sites, ad networks, e-commerce sites, file sharing sites and directories.

If you do not want to have limited budget, then specify upfront with "even delivery clause". This will ensure that your hits will be disseminated throughout the day without the publisher bringing you artificial volume of traffic all at once. So, take a look at chapter 7 of this book and identify the advertising networks you want to check out and see what they have on offer.

Outsourcing to Leverage Your Time

For every business owner whether online or offline, time management is very important. The success of your business greatly depends on your skills in managing the tasks within the available time. As for the individuals who work hard online, making it a part of their system will ease their duties such as in SEO, content writing, advertising and many more. However, the chances that you can outsource or delegate some of these tasks will depend on your achievement in the future and the status of your business. When it comes to some very important tasks which you cannot do alone, you will just have to pay someone to do the backlinking, article submissions and forum commenting. At the same time, this will pose a great advantage to you and your business because you can focus more on very important things such as marketing and advertising. This could help you to lead your business to the road of success. If you intend to delegate some of your tasks, the person that you appoint to do this for you should be reliable. Verify whether the person possess the skills needed to accomplish the assignments satisfactorily and above standard in due time. Although there are many job seekers or services online, not all can render quality in their work. With this, your contractor should have a better understanding on the field of online marketing. Take note that you still have to constantly monitor the progress of your project since there are instances that they lose track of their work. Instruct them to contact you whenever there are problems met to prevent future problems becoming a reality. SEO can be one of the tedious jobs online. It will cover a broad range of tasks such as article writing, social bookmarking and article submission. Nevertheless, be cautious whenever you outsource SEO work. However, there is still the option that you learn what SEO is all about and cover the job. SEO is one intricate job that will require a comprehensive knowledge. Therefore, an expert can be your best option to accomplish your project especially when you do not want to learn about SEO. The question now is where can you find one?

In the online business, you can build connections with other people. With this, you can use the opportunity to ask for recommendations especially in forums where people usually discuss about various aspects of online marketing. They might know someone who is an expert on a particular field. Chapter 7 will also cover businesses that provide such services.

Outsourcing a job is something not to be afraid of. It is only through this approach that you can get the job done with better and exceptional results. There is no need for you to learn everything especially when you can afford to pay a professional. It would then be easy for you to allocate your attention to other areas of your business and facilitate its expansion.

Hiring a Virtual Assistant

Contrary to most beliefs, success in business does not happen overnight. It will require dedication, hard work and commitment. If these are manifested consistently, earning a six-figure income is likely to be expected just like the successful marketers and entrepreneurs known in the online business world. However, the success is not only attributed to business owners. You also owe gratitude to the virtual team who has accomplished their duties with efficiency and dedication.

Besides, having a virtual team can greatly contribute to your online business at a low cost while you will be able to generate high sales and leads.

With this, you have done your workers a favor as well as your business.

Virtual teams possess a unique nature. Each member may have a different time zone, characteristics and nationality. Nevertheless, it is important for you to figure out their locality and allowable time to make a response or reports.

This will get the tasks done within the time given; thus, no hassles along the way.

Since you benefit from this kind of team structure, any dealings have to be emphasized. It is also imperative that you contact your employees in remote locations and notify them in advance whenever there are things to be done.

In this team, you are the head and the project manager, you should improve your managing skills to accomplish a set of tasks and eventually meet your goals. Since you will hire workers who are freelance in nature, you have to set deadlines for them to submit their assignments. Doing so will keep the team's work flowing smoothly and effectively. Ensure that they are accountable for their tasks. Once you keep doing this and maintaining consistency throughout, success is a big possibility.

You have to ensure that communication is vital in this type of venture. Therefore, you have to focus on effective communication with each other. Be transparent and convey your message with clarity. Doing so will prevent misunderstandings between you and your virtual assistants. Keeping the communication at regular interval is the responsibility of the team leader. Whatever it is that may happen or change in your company, it is very important that you keep your team informed. For decision-making, involve your employees since they are part of the team and this will give them a sense of belonging and responsibility.

If you are going to ask how this could be achieved, then let us presume that you are going to launch a product in the market and yet, you haven't still come up with the product name. In this situation, you can ask for recommendations from your team.

The virtual team and the processes involved will directly affect your online business. However, each one has to remember that hard work and dedication are the keys to a successful venture. In the long run, you can learn anything and with this, you will have to start somewhere. With consistency, it will not take you long before you see promising results.

Finding Unique Ways to Delight Your Customers

Your business needs a huge number of prospective buyers and customers. If that is then your goal, you can ask for their e-mails in exchange for free items. After all, you just have to follow potential customers until they are interested in your services or buying your products. The above mentioned strategy could be the most used in the world of online business and e-commerce. However, its meaning has changed remarkably since most consumers and businesses are now becoming value conscious. It is evident with this situation: when a product is not cheap, they will not buy it. It only makes sense that you give FREE stuff for your prospects to opt-in for your future marketing as part of the strategy. One of the best known strategies seen online is the use of free ebook. Your target customers simply have to download the free ebook on various niches of interest such as how to lose weight, ways to save money and many more that could catch the interest of your customers. An example of this is the CDBaby that sells CDs for independent musicians. As they offer free ebooks, they also promote careers on YouTube, Phone Apps, software, cheap items and ring tones as these also appeal to the interested market. This kind of strategy can pull a lot of prospective customers to you. The tendency is that people who bought products from you will buy repeatedly. With such in mind, an online business owner can promote their products and allow them to be remembered in a very unique way. Among the favorite things that people like are the promotional items such as pens, refrigerator magnets and coffee mugs that are typically seen every day. They are given for free and it never fails to catch the attention of the audience. On your website, you can invite customers to join your 'club'. It will give them the advantage of finding great and superb deals from your online business that cannot be found in the public. There are also opportunities to start a VIP network where the business itself offers the dedicated consumers access to new and exciting products, special items discount that are not available elsewhere and on low prices. This kind of marketing strategy appeals to a huge number of consumers. As a result, they will keep rushing and coming back to your website. There are also other strategies that will make customers buy on an impulse. Apart from the free giveaways, you can offer to do tasks like creating ads for a very cheap price for as low as $5, €5 or £5. In return, you could end up creating many ads or massive returns of customers that will buy other expensive services from your.

Having Competitive Prices on Your Products

Online business offers opportunities where you can use comprehensive analysis to understand the strategies used in your competitor businesses which may include their strengths and weaknesses, market share, strategies, niche area, foreseeable threats and opportunities.

The main objective of any businesses is success. However, it will be a complete struggle especially when you do not even lay out a plan to your success in this online business.

The internet has become a huge market place. Anyone from different geographical areas is not restricted from doing business online. In fact, it provides an equal opportunity for both small businesses and corporate companies.

You would probably ask why there are successful businesses while others are not successful. Why do customers have preferences when it comes to business to deal with? The answers to these questions could be answered after you have obtained proper competitor intelligence.

Since success is not the only destination of a business, competitive intelligence becomes a necessity if the owner will want to make his business stand out from the others. In fact, many online businesses fail because they are ignorant of the dynamic corporate setting and likewise clueless about who their competitors are or what they are doing to succeed. So what does the competitive analysis cover? Check the following key points:

Nature of Competition: When you are in this venture, it is imperative that you know who your competitors are. You should have information about their business volume, number of competitors, product mix and many more. You should also be aware of the quality of their services and the products they market to their target audience.

Market Analysis: Apart from the online business, entrepreneurs also have offline businesses. In fact, their online business partially supplements their offline business at which the former has its shares with sales and publicity. An example of this could be investment in real estate.

Studying the market will pose a competitive advantage to your business.

It is also important that you include pricing, marketing strategy, target customers or market, product presentation and information.

SWOT: The acronym SWOT stands for Strengths, Weaknesses, Opportunities and Threats. Having this information at hand, you will be knowledgeable enough on the strengths and weaknesses of any business. It will also provide you with relevant information about the available opportunities and foreseeable threats.

Competitive Websites: Included in the competitor intelligence, you should also study the websites of your competitors. These may include their layout, theme, links, design, ease of navigation and website's content.

The huge challenge for any kinds of businesses is to demonstrate how their products or services are different from others. A line is drawn to give the customers a full view of distinction from the others.

A competitive strategy can be formulated only after one has gained understanding of the competitors. In these times, it becomes a necessity for any kind of business to conduct a thorough competitive analysis not only during starting up a business but as well as when you are already on the business arena. This will help you build up a competitive edge.

To come up with a competitive analysis, one of the primary requirements is a detailed competitive intelligence. To accomplish such task, a professional should carry out a long research and has the capability to do a competitive analysis with clients.

Showcasing Customer Reviews

One of the powerful tools that you can use to your advantage is the reviews from your customers. In fact, it can significantly affect the click-through rates from the Search Engine Results Page (SERPS) plus the conversion rate of your website. Optimizing your online business website is part of the marketing strategy. It is pivotal to any kind of business since it can help you boost sales and visibility through an organic search. Since there are thousands of people who search online, you can now deliver your products and services with ease and efficiency. To give you a better understanding, the review can improve your status in SEO while at the same time giving you some tips on how you can maximize this opportunity. Reviews add unique, user generated content to your website. The search engines always use unique and new content. When you have collected diverse reviews, videos, photos and ratings, the search engine has enough reason to come back to you and index your website again. If your website is full of reviews, experiences of real users are shared with your prospective customers. Insights are provided to facilitate decision-making whenever the clients are about to buy a particular product and evaluate the business' services. Besides this, it can also help enrich the company. Videos and social media referrals improve your websites search-ability. The rich media content from clients has been proven to have an invisible link with the business' total sales. With this, you can encourage your potential customers to upload videos and photos. The algorithms of the search engines have drastically changed over the years. Presently, more importance is placed on social activity. When your website have more shares, likes and 1+, the search-ability is greater than usual. With this in mind, you have to ensure that the reviews should include advanced social sharing tools to major social media network. Reviews improve click through rates from search. The click-through rates are remarkably improved with product reviews. This is because the people are magnetized to results that have gold stars due to the following reasons: The stars indicate that it included reviews from real users and in turn, 63% of customers are likely to buy your products and available services when it has user reviews. When it has gold stars, the website itself appears to be trustworthy. Consequently, there will be trust that will help your online business to make more sales. The click-through rates from SERP's can be increased from 10% to 20%.

The Power of Spiritual, Emotional, Mental & Physical Well Being on Your Business

Are there things that you want in life like good health? Do you want to have a stable romantic relationship? How about more money? If you do not want anything, then this page is not for you. The reality of life is that it is not all the same for everybody. There are individuals who can get anything they want while there are others who are struggling hard just to achieve it. As for the former, they keep a low profile and hidden for obvious reasons.

Apart from such fate, traits are also diverse. Indeed each one is unique and it is just proven by the people's behavior and action. There are individuals who are good at showing results and achieving goals while others are not.

When the traditionally minded people first hear that manifesting and achieving one's goal is possible, they are deliberately surprised with the statement. There is no obvious reason that you cannot manifest or achieve your goals. I will assert that such is possible since I personally achieve my goal in life just like other people who have experienced success in life. You just have to make it your goal to achieve your goal.

Since this is a special topic, I will share with you one of the secrets to success. It is called the 'law of attraction.' You can incorporate it into your life to manifest those results you desire in life. With the law of attraction, it simply means that anything can be drawn to oneself.

To start with, there are three key points that you need to follow and agree. These may include:

Circumstances Determined by Beliefs: The first one is that circumstances are determined by beliefs because what we have accepted about the world is true, as far as we are concerned. An example of this is the saying that 'the road to success is through commitment and hard work.'

Sources of Beliefs: Furthermore, the beliefs that we have learned or practice today comes from our parents, society, education, peers, environment, personal experiences, etc.

Einstein once said that everything that vibrates is made up of energy. Therefore, there could either be a positive energy or a negative energy. If you want to achieve a positive result, it is always better to hang out with positive minded people and if you want to achieve a negative result, you hang out with negative people. Which one would you prefer? What if everything you have learnt in the past is partially incorrect?

That means that you are probably suffering today as a result of incorrect beliefs.

A good example of this is that most times, our parents tell us to go to the university and when we come out, we should look for a job to do. You hardly hear parents say when you come out of the university, 'Please start your own business.' You can now see how beliefs play a role in what happens to us in life. With this type of belief, common sense should prevail and not be suppressed like how the traditional people think.

Energy is Never-ending: Lastly, the energy is continuously dynamic and it never stops. So when we need to start over, we can do it anytime. Moreover, it is up to us on how we can harness the energy in motion. Just like what Einstein has shown, everything is composed of energy and they do vibrate. With this, we can attract the same vibrations. For instance, negative people yield negative results whereas, positive people harvest positive results. If you have fallen into the former type of person, then hang out with positive individuals to be influenced.

Since strong beliefs are a requirement to attain one's desired goals in life, how can a person have such conviction when he is already instilled with ingrained beliefs? The beliefs can be straightened through the five approaches which are the evidence, experiences, education, reason and emotion.

Generating strong beliefs means there is evidence. In this approach, spiritual manifestation comes into picture. I can cite proofs in my life such as the occurrences of wishful events that just happened at the right time.

To better understand Spiritual Manifestation, there are three essential key points that should come to your senses.

These will include the conscious mind, subconscious mind and the body that are obviously interconnected with one another.

Conscious Mind: Among the three parts, it is the conscious mind that thinks and reasons out. It can accept and reject any idea after thorough analysis. Then, whatever it is that we think about, determines our lives especially when we reject negative thoughts. However, the conscious mind has its limitation. The processing power can only accommodate 4096 bits of information per second. Furthermore, the conscious mind is also the origin of pain and pleasure.

Subconscious Mind: On the other hand, the subconscious mind cannot reject any thought. No matter what the conscious mind have accepted either good or bad, the subconscious mind simply accepts. However, this part surpasses the conscious mind since it works throughout the body making it the centre power of existence.

Moreover, it can accommodate larger bits of information which can amount to more than 4 megabits. This only means that it can store more information than the conscious mind. It is noted that the subconscious mind works throughout the body. It expresses itself through feelings and actions. Contrary to the traditional people's belief, making revisions and rewrite about beliefs and incorporating behavior is now made easier with energy-based psychology.

Body: We do not exist primarily because of the body. Instead, it is the mind that is the mode of existence. The body is simply an instrument or vehicle for the mind to interact with the material world. When we manifest our desires through physical action, the body is controlled with collective beliefs that consequently build a barrier for the mind to manifest our desires.

To put the insights into action and put law of attraction into effect, focusing on a particular goal is the key. Once you focus on it, a conscious thought is created that will eventually be accepted by the subconscious mind. Since the latter expresses actions, the result will be manifested by the body whereby it will work towards the goal and this will serve as a basis to keep us focused. However, when we focus on unwanted results, then we are likely to reap what we have sowed.

In situations where we asked for something, we have to ask for it in a friendly and worry-free manner.

There should be an attitude of expectation and once apprehensions are noted, it will only show that you lack faith. As a result, you will not get what you want.

Lack of faith draws the line of limitation. It gets in the way that will eventually hinder you from achieving the things or events that you want to see happen. It only makes sense to say that when you ask for something from a position of lack of belief, you will never have it.

The manifestation usually comes in different forms where we less likely expected it. Many of us look for results everywhere but it is disguised as something else right in front us. For instance, you are asking the universe to give you a million dollar from a lottery. However, the manifestation is evident in a business opportunity which you may have come across.

To make it simple, manifestations will depend on the person who aims to make a difference and achieve his desires in life. Since Quantum principles have just unraveled its secrets, it facilitates one's achievement. With this, our conscious thoughts become beliefs when it reaches our subconscious mind and will eventually be manifested in the physical world. However, it is of utmost importance that we eradicate wrong beliefs and replace it with profound ones. With this, it will be a start of a better fulfilling life destiny.

Recognizing Business Risks and Understanding How to Deal With Them

When people are facing difficulties in life, they tend to have nowhere to go to other than to find solutions to those problems. Just like in business, challenges are anticipated and faced.

Since you do not have any idea about the chances of unwanted events happening in your online business especially when you have not started generating good cash flow, developing a Plan B is imperative. This is important especially when you are going to launch the business, new services and products. It will just serve as an alternative means in order for your business to survive.

However, if you are already in the process of failing in your business, then the time is just ripe for you to develop a different plan that will potentially serve as an exit strategy. When your online business is in the midst of crisis, always look for things inside your business that will work better if repositioned effectively. With such dreadful business events, you should always stay prepared since anything can happen in just a matter of time.

Reaching Out to Potential Partners

You often hear success stories from individuals who earned millions in just 2 days. With this kind of story or statement, will it not stir curiosity? In fact, many individuals get puzzled on how situations like this can change their lives over night. Nevertheless, the answer is in Joint Venture (JV) opportunities. If you are unfamiliar with the term, it is most likely you will ask, "What is a joint venture?" To answer the question, it simply refers to partnership between business owners for the attainment of their goals. In this project, more sales are generated for each business since the profit is divided. In case you are new to this field, you will surely enjoy the process and the financial opportunity it can bring to your online business. If you have your own business and new ideas which you want to implement, it becomes difficult sometimes to implement them on your own. However, if you have a joint venture partnership, it will keep you inspired throughout to get the tasks done. With this, you can have new products or services in the market immediately. Take note that joint venture opportunities could parachute you up to the 'mountain of fortune.' Finding a big joint venture partner starts from the small ones. In the long run, it will help get you up the ladder and the key to ceasing opportunities for big joint ventures is participation in small joint ventures. There is a great advantage when you get involved in a joint venture. It will push you to give and do your best in this competitive market. Consequently, if your JV partner likes your project, he can include your product in his list and that will eventually bring success to your business sales. To impress your JV partner, you will inevitably have to push your limits and sharpen your skills. When you reach that level, chances of you being mentioned or promoted is high. As a result, you will be invited again, get promoted and recommended while your products and services are at the forefront. With this, many people will buy from you since you are highly recommended by well-known partners. In online business, participating and learning about joint venture opportunities is considered to be the fastest way to boost your sales. It is a different kind of venture yet, it will give you promising real results. With this in mind, I hope you will today start searching and contacting potential partners within your target market.

Using Press Releases to Help Your Small Business

Competing with other businesses is indeed a big hurdle to overcome. However, there are still many ways for you to keep up or surpass other businesses. It can be through your effective marketing strategies or any other ways. So what are the strategies or tools that can be used? Examples of this is opting for press releases and working on the aspects at which your competitors seemingly neglect. If that is the case, there is the need to fully understand the corporate world you are in and come up with effective marketing strategies. Going to the main point, press releases has been around for a long time within businesses. With such length of existence, some people think of it as a stale promotional option that can only be used in newspapers and radio. By looking at a different perspective, press releases can still be an effective tool to promote your business as well as your products and services. It can be distributed effectively using the internet as its platform. In just a matter of time, its reach is beyond what you have expected. Although the press releases are best distributed online, still, this promotional tool will not be enough. It will call for proper and efficient distribution. So how are you going to distribute a press release? Since you are using a press release as part of your marketing strategy, it would be best if you will distribute it through a press release tool. Sign up for membership as this will give you the opportunity to use other additional tools that will give you the edge over other competitors.

Chapter 4
Marketing Through Branding

<u>In This Chapter</u>

Why Branding is Very Important for Your online Business

Generating Leads through Branding

Improving Sales through Branding

The Importance of Brand Advocacy

Why Brand Insistence is Best for Your Business

Focusing on Your Target Market

Building a Brand That Changes With Time

Creating a Personality for Your Brand

Why Branding is Very Important for Your Online Business

Having a brand would only be beneficial to any business if potential customers are aware of it as well as the characteristics and qualities that are associated or linked with it. Brand awareness refers to the way of determining or identifying a brand through its logo and offered services. A brand is not just a name of a business or product. It is a factor that helps people in deciding whether to buy a particular product or not. A brand contributes when it comes to ranking a product in the market. A strong, powerful, and popular brand always helps in making a product get a higher rank in the marketplace.

Brand Advocacy: This involves people talking about your brand all the time and customers or lovers of your brand are always on the lookout for what your next product will be. A typical example of a company with this type of branding is Apple Inc.

Brand Preference: People always have a preferred brand for almost everything, and it is called "brand preference." Brand reputation influences consumer's brand preference most of the time. The main reason why buyers prefer to choose one brand over its competitors is because they like the characteristics and features that are associated with that brand.

Brand Equity: Brand equity refers to the value that is associated with a brand. It is not really easy to assess the value of a particular brand because its equity is often perceived by the consumers.

Brand Recall: Brand recall refers to the ability of the customers to recall or remember the characteristics and other unique details that are associated with a brand. This is the main reason why advertisers often repeat phrases or advertisement lines to promote their products.

Brand Insistence: In brand insistence, quality is guaranteed. A successful brand always assures its buyers with an implicit quality level. Most of the time, the consumers distinguish the quality level of a product based on its brand.

Dynamic Branding: Branding may constantly change. Every time a customer interacts with a brand, his or her opinion on that brand might change. So, such interactions should always be positive to obtain a long lasting customer relationship. It is also advisable that you consider branding through achievements, branding by association with the right people and branding by testimonial from clients and others.

Brand Extension: Brand extension refers to the process of taking an established brand and improving it to produce a new product. This process is crucial. The new product will surely catch the attention of consumers when it hits the marketplace. However, if it gets many negative feedback and reviews, the credibility of the entire brand will be damaged eventually. Branding helps in comparing products. Learn how to use it to come up with your own product in the niche of your choice.

Brand Positioning: Many business entrepreneurs are good at developing business plans. They know exactly how to address the product and operational issues of their businesses. In some cases, the business plans that small business owners made compete with the business plans of big time brands. However, the most common factor that makes small businesses left behind by the bigger ones is marketing. In this part, we will discuss the ways on how to market your online business just like a big brand through a process called "brand positioning".

Often, small business owners do not market their products the way large business owners do because they usually fail to obtain real brand positioning. Brand positioning should be understood as identifying a brand's biggest advantage against its most powerful competitors and among its most promising targets.

The problem with small businesses is that they only address one of those major key aspects. They either focus on their target market only or on their competitors only. In order for you to market a small business like a big brand, you should think of an effective way in addressing both key aspects.

Online business owners need to plan for a "fertile competition." They need to know which businesses are doing well in the market. They also need to determine which competitors they can 'steal' some market shares from. That is exactly how huge brands think every time. They always analyze the performance of big brands in the market before attacking them. If you want to market a small business like a big one, you need to learn from the huge brands out there.

The second key factor that small business owners should consider is the most promising target market. Small businesses need to learn how to analyze their target market.

Big time businesses usually spend much time in analyzing their target market. They only focus on a specific niche.

Most of the time, big brands analyze their target markets demographically and psycho-graphically. They also look for a target market that can be perfectly captured by their products or services. If they think that their product does not fit their target market, they take action in developing new products or services that would be suitable for that target market.

Generally, brand positioning refers to the company's advantage against a specific group of competitors and among a group of target audience that are suitable for your product.

Brand positioning requires good time for analysis and research, but its results are extremely rewarding. Small businesses might experience some downfalls during the process, but that is fine. They will surely learn from those mistakes. Establishing and maintaining a good brand positioning is one of the best ways on how to market a small business like a big brand.

Businesses spend much money every year for branding their products and services. They spend money for literature, in manufacturing their products, and advertising them on websites. The main idea of branding is to give your products unique identities that will make them stand out and become recognizable in your target market.

If you do not want to put efforts in handling your promotional branding effectively, your target consumers might not be aware of your products and just ignore them.

Consumers might also get confused with your products and mistake them for your competitors' products. There is a way on how to avoid this.

You need to make improvements with your promotional branding. Do not just focus on the physical appearance or design of the product.

You need to come up with a new brand that your target consumers will trust and love to use repeatedly.

The most important thing that a business should always consider is their target audience. Do you intend to sell your products to young women? Do you want to sell them to teenagers? Do you want to sell them to older men? Knowing your target audience will help you hit the most appropriate note in advertising your products.

Once you have already figured out your target audience, you need to ensure that you present your brand to them properly and effectively. You need to come up with innovative and unique methods that will help you in marketing your products successfully. You may promote an event where you can feature your products. You may build a website for your business. You may create social media pages where you can interact with your target audience and keep them updated with your latest products and services.

You may also hire a very popular and influential person to endorse your products. Never ever get shy in promoting your own brand because you need to get the attention and interest of as many people as possible to get your products recognized and remembered.

Take note that creating a new brand for a particular target audience and promoting it constantly may be time consuming and difficult to manage, so you might need to hire additional staff to do these for you.

Branded Image: A customer buys a product based on his or her emotion and justifies it with logic. Believe it or not, the image of your brand has the power to set the tone for that emotion. If it tells your target audience that you are the best provider of the product that they need, then they will be confident to buy your products and services. You need to earn the trust of your target audience in order for your business to become successful.

How to Identify Your Branded Image: It is very important for a business to identify what exactly its brand represents. If you are a freelancer and you want to market yourself to prospective clients, you should first list down the benefits that they might get for hiring you. You may also list your experiences and proven track record.

You also need to know what your edge over your competitors is and vice versa. Compare your qualities to their qualities and check out the qualities that your target audience is looking for. You will know that you have already established a branded image for yourself if you have exhibited your qualities and experiences well, if you find a way on how to promote yourself that your rivals can compete against, and if your target audience has decided to stop dealing with your competitors.

Branding Through Design: Branding by design will also be helpful to you. You may create your own business cards, posters, brochures, pocket folders, and flyers to advertise your services. If graphic design is not your strength, you may simply hire an amazing graphic designer to do the job for you.

Always remember that your own brand makes you unique and stand out among your competitors. When you brand yourself right, you will surely get higher returns than what you have invested.

Generating Leads through Branding

All businesses put efforts in generating leads. One of the most excellent ways to do this is through excellent content marketing. Here are some of the powerful tips for content marketing. Your company website should provide all necessary information about your business. Each webpage should convey a valuable message so its content should be great, specific, straight to the point, and easy to understand.

Keep in mind that readers tend to get bored when reading a huge block of text, so you need to make the content of your website concise and short without missing any important details about your business.

The tune of your content should be based on the buying stage of your prospective buyers. You should use some intelligent marketing automation systems that will help you determine the activities of your website visitors. Content strategy should focus on the buyers and researchers who want to get information about your products and services.

If you have a worldwide target audience, you should never forget to provide multiple language support on your website. In that way, you can provide the same information to people of all nationalities. If you want to attract your website audience effectively, you should consider posting other types of content like product reviews, client testimonials, product demos, research reports, white papers, and other support documents.

Basic content guidelines can also be applied to Business-to-Business (B2B) content marketing strategy. These guidelines or rules include usage of simple words, attention-grabbing titles, SEO-friendly and bulleted content, audio content, video content, user-friendly navigation options, and attractive call-to-action buttons.

Since communication is one of the most important keys in any type of business, you should encourage your visitors to connect with you. You may create a form that they can fill-up to send as a feedback. If you want to get more visitors to your site, you should add a feature that will enable visitors to share your website content in social media sites.

Nowadays, social media plays a very important role in lead generation. In the field of social media marketing, business owners should listen to the comments and suggestions of their current customers and target audience. They should update their social media pages regularly so that they can constantly monitor client interactions. You can use their comments and include the content that you have posted on your website.

When you share your content through social media sites, you need to make sure that it redirects the readers to your website or to other beneficial content. In that way, you will be able to evaluate the priorities, needs, and interest levels of your site visitors.

With content and social media marketing, lead generation can be done in a quick, easy and more effective way.

Improving Sales through Branding

In the field of Internet marketing, the brand that a particular business has established would be its identity in the online community. If you want to promote your business through Internet marketing, you should first come up with a brand that will stand out among its competitors. You might need to put extra effort and time in doing this because it is not easy to stand out on the Internet because it has a very wide range. You will also need to be specific when choosing your niche.

Here are the guidelines that will help you in branding your online business effectively.

You need to come up with a great logo for your business. It has already proven that most people tend to recall visual images than business names. So, you need to make a logo that will act as the visual representation of your online business. A logo can also help you set your own trademark and make your target audience recognize your business more effectively.

Most people, including your target audience, are into social networking nowadays. So, it would be easier for you to inform them about the updates in your business by connecting to them through different social media sites. Every time you post content on your business' social media page, it will instantly be posted to the content feed of your prospective customers.

Do not take advantage of this by posting low quality content. You need to make sure that every piece of information that you post is valuable to your readers and relevant to your business at the same time. Using high traffic social media sites like Facebook, Twitter, Google + and Pinterest would be ideal for spreading information and news about your business. Do not forget to link your social media accounts so that once content is posted, it goes to the other social media pages of your business.

Advertising is a powerful method that will help you in promoting your products and services on the web. It will also help you in making people aware of your brand and business. You may write a press release about your new brand or business and use viral marketing tools in spreading announcements and information that defines your brand.

These are just some of the best ways in establishing your brand on the web. Once you establish a brand online, it would be easier for your target audience to recognize your business and build long-term business relationships with your clients.

The Importance of Brand Advocacy

Brand ambassadors are involved in any brand advocacy. They are advanced professionals who are considered experts in catching the interest of any target audience. Their job is to create a huge buzz that can generate powerful and effective word-of-mouth advertising.

Brand advocacy may also involve different street psychology techniques that are applied to control the mental shifts in your client base. This process will help you save time in branding your business.

Brand ambassadors are usually selected based on the products or services that should be promoted. They are also known as endorsers or product models. They are usually the trendsetters who have the power to attract people's attention and persuade them to use the product or service that they endorse.

Brand ambassadors consist of influential people who can instill acceptance and trust in the minds of your target audience, increase your ROI (Return on Investment), decrease the necessary branding time for your business, generate effective word-of-mouth advertising, get people talking about the message of your business.

Since brand ambassadors can generate the most powerful advertising type ever (word-of-mouth), you do not need to get a billboard. Their service fees are even more affordable than the cost of a billboard. Offline marketing professionals specialize in street psychology.

Here are some of the advertising mediums that brand ambassadors use in driving business messages deep into the minds of the target audience.

- Advocacy
- Bikes/cars
- Trucks/lorries/buses
- Publicity stunts
- Scooters

Successful marketing companies use their brand ambassadors to engage a synergistic, dual focused and multi-channeled approach to their marketing strategies. Even though the costs are less expensive, the results are still amazing. The advertising mediums that marketing companies employ are always designed to grab attention. Most of the time, expert marketing account managers collaborate with brand ambassadors to make a business' message get instantly accepted by the target audience.

These professionals are the essential components that will help your business succeed. If you are looking for amazing ROI results for your business, you always need to consider applying revolutionary approaches in your marketing strategies. Using brand ambassadors is a very smart decision if you want your brand to get noticed by your target audience quickly. You will surely be stunned once you see how beneficial they are to your business. They can make you richer.

Why Brand Insistence is Best for Your Business

The success of every business depends on what we call "Brand Insistence." This is the ultimate goal all businesses aim at. Businesses will only be able to make more money from their products if their target audience buy and use their products regularly. Brand insistence refers to the commitment of the consumers to a particular brand. The term implies that a customer is not only after the benefits that he or she gets, but also willing to return something to the brand. It is reflected in word-of-mouth advocacy or by referring the brand to other people who might also be interested in it.

What Brand Insistence Implies: Repurchasing of a particular product is not really the best determining factor of brand insistence. There are cases when customers buy a particular product repeatedly because there are no other alternatives or the best ones are not always available. It is not brand insistence but "spurious loyalty." Brand insistence is definitely more than just false loyalty. It can only become possible once a company or business was able to create a successful emotional attachment between their target market and their product. Obtaining brand insistence from consumers might take some time, but it will really become a great asset to any company.

Why Customers Develop Brand Insistence: Brand insistence refers to the customers' decision in buying a particular product that is usually expressed through their behavior to that product. A consumer usually develops insistence for a brand simply because he or she thinks that it offers high quality products for reasonable prices. Customers will only be encouraged to buy products or services if they think that they offer relevance and value to them.

What Can Influence Brand Insistence: There are several things that can influence brand insistence like product design, tag line writing, and understanding what the customer needs. Brand insistence will occur once the customers recognize a brand in a positive way. Developing and maintaining insistence among customers is really important for every type of business. So, a business owner should make sure that the customers will have good impression of the brand that they promote. You need to be aware that every customer always makes a trial purchase for every product that catches their attention. If they are satisfied with the product, they will surely repurchase it.

Mindset of a Brand Loyalist: A consumer who is already loyal to a particular brand has a mindset of his or her own. Since he or she is committed to the brand or product, he or she tends to repurchase and use it. Customers are willing to pay more for a product or brand that conveys all the characteristics that they prefer or features that are valuable to them. So, if you want to get loyal buyers, you need to ensure the quality of your brand. Happy customers always recommend their favorite products to their family, friends, and colleagues.

The Importance of Brand Insistence: Brand insistence is very important for a business because it acts as the determinant of the sale of a brand. Since the companies today are very competitive, you need to make your business survive by keeping up with your competitors. You should never ever lose customers. Having many customers who trust your brand will result to a dramatic improvement to your business. Customers who insist on your products will tend to be less sensitive to price increase because they are willing to pay more in exchange of a product that has constant high level of quality. Once you get an established brand with a huge customer base, you will never need to spend much money for advertising purposes. You will just wait for more sales to come.

How to Create and Maintain Brand Insistence: Creating brand insistence might require more time than maintaining it. First, you need to come up with a high quality product that can address the needs of your target market. You should always keep the price of your product reasonable. Never forget to inform your customers about the value or importance of their purchase. Once you have established a stable customer base, you need to improve your business' customer services so that you will be able to interact and connect with your customers. In that way, you will be able to know their comments and suggestions that will help you improve your brand and products.

Focusing on Your Target Market

Online brand development is a very important strategy to help your target customers to recognize your business as well as your products and their uses. Online branding can also help your business build a reputation and gain popularity.

You need to be aware that business branding cannot be done in just 24 hours. It may take more time to employ all the strategies that you have planned.

Before developing any branding strategies, a business should first determine the brand that they should promote. They need to analyze their target market well in order for them to come up with the right brand that will make them become successful in the future. The brand of a business represents its quality and reliability.

Here are 5 of the most important questions that you need to answer before determining the right branding strategy for your products.

What You Do: You need to know the products and services that you are going to offer. You also need to come up with the terms and conditions of your business. You need to determine how your product works in order for you to correctly identify the right brand for it.

What Sets You Apart: You need to know the unique qualities of your product that makes it different or better than its competitors.

Why Would Customers Care: In this part, you need to determine how your product can have an impact on or change the quality of life of your customers.

Why Would Customers Buy from You: You need to identify the reasons why your customers should use your product and why they would use it regularly.

What Your Strengths & Weaknesses Are: It is very important for you to identify the strengths and weaknesses of your product. You need to know the limitations of your product as well as its qualities that will be helpful to your target customers.

Online business branding will help your business become more reputable and recognizable. It is an effective strategy that will help you improve your ability to extend your business on the internet. Here are some of the most powerful strategies that will help you in focusing on your target market effectively:

Add More Topics on Your Official Website: Free advertisement sites will only permit you to submit your site to only one relevant category. Adding more subjects to your website will allow you to submit it to many free ad sites.

Increase your product value by making rare special offers: You may increase limit time for bonuses, promos, and discounts.

Take Time to Identify Your Competitors: Learn more about what they do and what they offer to their customers.

Identify Your Niche Market and Sell Your Products There: You should also identify your target audience or customers.

Make Series of Advertising and Marketing Tests: You will save time, effort, and money by promoting your offers to the right group of customers.

Use the "Fortune Teller" Strategy: In persuading your visitors to buy your products, you need to tell them how your product can change their lives.

Customers Always Love to Get Free Items: It is a great idea to give away some trial products to your target customers for a limited time. Do not forget to ask for their comments about your products. You may do this step before launching your products in the market.

Create Multiple Websites That Will Lead Your Target Customers to Your Main Site: You may create review sites that will contain links to your official business site. Creating multiple websites will help in improving your search engine ranking.

Let Your Target Audience Know That You Have Already Built a Website for Your Business: You may inform them about your latest products, promos, discounts, or freebies through using an e-mail list.

Do Not Use the Same Banner Ads Repeatedly: You need to design new banners from time to time. Use the right fonts, colors, and logos that will catch the interest of your target audience to visit your website.

Make Sure That Your Website Loads Faster: You can do this by decreasing banner ads on it. You may use buttons instead of banners because they can help you save more space on your site.

Joint Venture with Reputable Businesses: You may also search some reputable companies and offer free advertising to them on your website. They might also offer you the same.

Offer Free Consultation: It is also ideal to offer free consultation via phone call to your clients. In that way, they will be able to know more about your business as well as your personality.

Philanthropy: You may search for a charity that your target audience might like to support. Do not forget to mention in your ad copy that you are going to share part of your business' profits to that charity.

Hold a Contest: You may tell your customers that the person who buys the most products will win a package that contains your greatest products or a full refund of their overall purchase. You may do this monthly, bi-monthly, or annually.

Network with Your Industry Key Players: Find some people who are popular in the industry and invite them to an interview. Ask their legal permission for the publication of the interview and use it to promote your site on different online magazines (e-zines).

Create a Product Review Website: Do not forget to build a testimonial or client review page on your website. Your clients would surely love to see their names on your website. Always encourage your clients to leave some reviews or testimonials regarding their experiences in using your products. You may also give them some rewards like electronic coupons that they can use to buy your products in the future.

Building a Brand That Changes with Time

Increasingly brands are using Twitter to connect with their clients nowadays. However, some of them are still not sure about the ways on how to increase their followers. Always keep in mind that quality business relationship is more important than the number of customers you have. It is because your client base will surely grow with the help of your loyal customers.

Here are the top 5 simple and quick steps that a brand should follow to increase its Twitter followers:

Post link: You need to make sure that your Twitter posts carry some links that will redirect your readers or followers to your site. You may also use links that redirect to your other social media accounts. By doing these, you will be able to connect with them using other platforms and get more prospective clients every time they share your links or posts to their own followers.

Offer Rewards: Brands that are using Twitter can easily gain followers by simply offering rewards or incentives. You tweet your followers and tell them that once your page gets

1000 followers, you will give them a chance to win a big prize.

Post Engaging Content: Brands need to ensure that the messages that they post to their sites are engaging, interesting, and relevant to the interests of their followers. You may tweet about some relevant issues, update about your new products, or some tips and advice that will help them in using some particular products.

Retweet: Choose tweets that might catch the interest of your readers and retweet them one by one. Always remember that you need to say five things about other people or brands for every one thing that you say about your brand.

Follow Friday Tag (#ff): The Follow Friday idea started in 2010 and it is used to suggest interesting companies or people that you are currently following and recommend to other Twitter users. It will be useful in making your target audience aware of your business as well as your products.

Market Research: Once you have successfully signed up with some reliable ad networks, the next thing that you should do is make sure that you are already familiar with the process of targeting audience for each campaign that you want to run. You may use different metrics which include age, household income, marital status, educational level, race, and gender. You also need to make sure that the demographics that you have listed for your offers perfectly match to the demographics of the websites that you advertise on.

Quantcast: Quantcast is definitely one of my favorite sites to do free demographic research. If you are not using any tool yet, you need to search for the one that works best for you. In addition, you can gather data from other websites that your visitors love to visit. In that way, you will be able to get some ideas about the types of promos and offers that they will love.

Google Ad Planner is a great alternative to Quantcast. However, some online marketers still prefer Quantcast over Google ad planner. You may use it if you want to have diversity when it comes to your market research sources. You can access it at Google Ad Planner.

Alexa: You can measure the overall traffic of a website by checking its Alexa rank. Please take note that any website that has an Alexa rank of less than 100,000 gets huge amount of traffic.

Quantcast uses Alexa to get information about its traffic data. Market Samurai has a combined power of Quantcast, Alexa, and Google Ad Planner. I definitely recommend it to you.

Compete: You can use Compete.com to check out the profiles of different websites. It gives very detailed breakdowns of unique number of visitors as well as other useful information. You have the chance to access better amount of information using the Compete Pro. However, it is not free of charge. You may be required to pay a fee.

You may use the "site tags" feature of Compete to generate a quick summary of websites that are related to your chosen broad market. It can give you great information regarding the best websites that you can promote with CPA offers.

Creating a personality for your brand

There is a step-by-step process in creating a company's brand personality. Of course, it involves the process of establishing a brand name, defining it, and promoting it.

Defining a Brand for Your Business: When creating a brand for your business, you need to come up with a visual representation for it. You need to choose the right font styles, background colors, or images that will make it stand out. Most corporate brands use traditional fonts and simple colors (like red or blue) for their logos. On the other hand, food brands usually use fun fonts and images as well as colors like yellow, black, and red. The visual representation of your brand would be of great help in defining your company's brand personality.

The visual representation of your brand would be of great help in defining your company's brand personality. It should appear on your website, vouchers, flyers, and advertisements. It also conveys the idea that your company is professional and serious in providing high quality products and services.

Differentiating Your Brand from Your Competitors: Next, you need to differentiate your brand from its competitors. You need to know the qualities and features that make your brand different and what makes it stand apart from its logo and name. You need to express the personality of your brand by using complex methods. This might involve online or print advertising. You may also create a press release that will link your readers to the solutions that you can offer to them. There is another effective and excellent way to express your brand personality and that is through creating a website. If you are running an online business, you should be specific in pointing out the qualities that are valuable to the people who buy your products. Is your product safe? Is it reliable? Is it affordable? How does your brand differ from other brands? If you are having trouble in making decisions regarding your brand personality, do not worry because it is natural. Some business owners really find it hard to identify their target audience. Always keep in mind that creating multifaceted brands is not really an effective and powerful strategy because it might cause confusion. You need to pick only one persona and focus on it. This strategy will help you come up with easier marketing strategies.

Chapter 5
On to the Search Engine Optimization: Understanding and using It Effectively

In This Chapter

Understanding Search Engines

Top Key SEO Checklist, Offsite and Onsite SEO

Keyword Ranking

Use of Inbound links and Content Based Backlinks

Page Ranking and Why You Need to Avoid Hard to Index Pages

Use of Webmaster Tools

Search Engine Listing Status

Search Engine Marketing (SEM)

Monitoring Your Competitors

Free Google Tools for Online Business

Understanding Searching Engines

Some people find it difficult to increase the search engine ranking of a website because search engines do not provide all information on how exactly they assess every website. However, one thing is for sure. All search engines use the same approach in assessing and collecting information from every website. To learn more about that approach, you need to get started with Search Engine Optimization (SEO). A search engine uses 3 different types of software which include Query software, Spider software, and Index software.

Spider Software: Each search engine uses unique spider software. However, all unique spider applications work similarly. They do "web crawling." You may visualize it by imagining a huge net that is being casted on the Internet. That net is being controlled and used by the spider software to collect all relevant links, texts, and URLs. Once the net has collected those details, the spider software will then pass them onto the so-called index software. You need to have patience when dealing with SEO. The spider software takes a while to collect all needed information from a website. You also need to give enough attention and focus on the links and URLs that it gathers and not just on the texts.

Index Software: Website owners always want their sites to become successful. They want to generate success not only for themselves but also for the company that they represent. In order for them to reach their goals, they need to understand the basics of search engine optimization as it serves as the most important factor that contributes to the success or failure of any website. Search engines operate according to their own set protocols or rules that they do not reveal completely to the public. Index software is used to take all information that the spider software has collected. It uses an algorithm in assessing information, determining its contents, and knowing its relevance to any type of search. Even though the public is not aware of the inner process of the index software, people understand that there are factors that are being valued by the search engines which include meta tags, keywords, and backlinks. You always need to focus on the information that your website gives to the index software that will make your search engine ranking increase. In this case, you need to focus on doing two important things: (A) know the types of information that the index software gathers from your website, (B) know the types of information that you want them to collect from your website so you will know how to adjust them.

Query Software: When a person thinks about a search engine, he or she usually come up with a misleading picture in his or her mind. When people think of Google, the contents that Google has pop up in their minds. Most of them think that it is already the search engine. No, it is not. The real search engine runs behind the interface that we all see. The user needs to communicate with the search engine through its interface, but he or she will never see how exactly it works. He or she will only see the results that it generated. The interface serves as the "face" of the engine, while the process that works behind it serves as its "brain." The query software does not collect website information on its own. When you type something on it, it just searches the so-called index software that is being run by the search engine. The index software collects all information from the spider software that the search engine also uses. What do all of these mean? To sum it all up, you should work backwards when you are analyzing a search engine. Always remember that it is the spider software that collects information from your website's text, URLs, and other links and the index software assesses all the information, defines the content of your site, and determines its relevance to a given search. Every time you build a website, you need to focus on the links, texts, and URLs that you want to be collected by the spider software in a way that the search engine's index software will rank your site for all relevant searches. Once you put all of these things together, with your knowledge about search engines and the tools that will make your website get higher rankings, your website will be able to show on the top results thus leading prospective customers to your website.

Top Key SEO Checklist, Offsite and Onsite SEO

Even if you are still a beginner when it comes to SEO strategies and techniques, you might realize that you really do not need to hire someone to do the job for you. However, you should not think that SEO is an extremely easy work. If you want to start optimizing your website for the search engines, you need to understand these basic elements:

Keywords: These are the words that you need to target so that your website will appear on search engine results whenever a person types them. If you want your keywords to be successful, then you must be very specific in choosing them. You should also focus on highly searched keywords and avoid the extremely competitive ones.

Meta tags: These are the tags that you put on your website. They are not visible to your visitors, but they are clearly visible to search engines. You can use tags to instruct the search engines and guide them about the things that they can find on your website.

Backlinks: These are links from other websites that redirect people to your own website. Every backlink that you get is equivalent to the so-called "vote of confidence" from any search engine. In other words, backlinks can contribute to increase the search engine ranking of your website. If you have finally decided to become more serious when it comes to search engine optimization, you need to take time in finding a tool that will play a vital role in making your website benefit from the 3 elements that were mentioned above. You need to look for a tool that will help you in maximizing your keyword usage, optimizing all of your meta tags, and building backlinks. Google keyword tool is one of the most recommended tools that will help you in doing all of that. Your SEO efforts will pay off with Google keyword tool and your basic knowledge about it. The higher the search engine ranking of your website is, the more sales it will generate. More sales mean more money.

Understanding On-Page Ranking Factors And What They Mean For You: In SEO, we refer to on-page ranking and off-page ranking. On-page ranking factors are the ones that you can fully control because they are already present on your website. On the other hand, off-page ranking factors cannot be found on your website so you only have less control over them.

Both on-page and off-page ranking factors are important for your website's search engine ranking. However, you should focus more on on-page ranking factors because they can give your website and your business immediate improvement.

The most important thing that you should always consider when it comes to dealing with on-page ranking factors is to do the right thing and avoid all wrong things. Of course, this will include your knowledge about what they right and wrong things are.

Understanding Off-Page Ranking Factors and What They Mean for You: When the search engines started to exist many years ago, the main thing that they have focused on was the content of the websites. When Google entered the scene, the usage of algorithms that involve links as part of the assessment also emerged. The said algorithm became really valuable to the search engine philosophy. As you know, the search engines have already prevented website owners from manipulating the search engine system. In this case, dealing with off-page facts became an ideal way to take some control out of the hands of the website owners.

You might now be wondering why you still need to deal with off-page SEO ranking factors if you do not have control over them. Well, you should first learn about the ways on how search engines operate. Once you do that, you will discover that you can still manipulate your off-page ranking factors even if you do not directly control them.

Why Title Tags are Essential: A website will not generate sales or traffic if its content is not good enough for its readers. In order for you to ensure that it will generate your desired amount of traffic, you need to do everything it takes to make it reach a higher ranking.

Keywords and backlinks are indeed important in search engine optimization, but you also need to focus on your title tags. Many people neglect a title tag because they are not aware of its real importance. You will notice that there is always a place for a title on every website. The title tag gives directions to search engine and helps it to determine how relevant the website is to the given search.

Here is an example. Let's say you own an agency called Apple Venture Travel Agency that is located in Los Angeles, California. If your title tag only includes "Apple Venture Travel Agency," your site might only show up in highly specific searches. If you put up something like "Apple

Venture Travel Agency: We Serve Los Angeles and All Surrounding Areas with Extremely Fast and Affordable Travel Discounts!" on your title tag, it will surely make you website rank higher in the following searches:

Traveling to Los Angeles

Traveling to Los Angeles and its surrounding areas

Cheapest Way to Travel to Los Angeles

Discounted flights to Los Angeles

As you can see, adding descriptive words in your title tag makes a big difference! You may also include title tags on separate pages of your website.

Keyword Ranking, Use of Inbound links and Content Based Backlinks

Keyword Ranking: You need to know the keywords that are searched frequently on search engines. You should be aware that there is a tough competition among keywords and each one is usually used more than the others.

Market Samurai can help you determine the keywords that have more searches and the keywords that can generate traffic on your website. You need to know all the possible search terms that people use to find products or services that are similar to what your company offers. You may create a detailed and comprehensive list of all relevant search terms as well as their rankings so that you will know which ones to use or avoid.

How would you know if a keyword should be used or avoided? First, choose the keywords that you think will obtain better results for your products. Next, determine the market that is most appropriate or suitable for your products on that market only.

Keyword Anchor Text - And Surrounding Text: In learning more about SEO, you need to understand what an anchor text is. It is the text that is part of every link.

You can use social media as a way to build backlinks, so you will need to provide the exact terms or words that your followers need to be able to share your site. You may also exchange links with other relevant websites, so you will need to tell them exactly the message that your links convey. When you write SEO articles and submit them using article submission uploader feature, you will be able to create links yourself.

Anchor texts are also used to share other items on your website. Even though search engines are constantly changing and evolving, they will always focus on the content of every website more than any other factors. Every time you make an anchor text, you need to make sure that it reflects on your keywords and the content that surrounds it.

Meta tags & Online Business: Meta tags are one of the most confusing elements of SEO, because they are multilayered unlike backlinks and keywords. To help you understand more what meta tags are, you only need to remember that they are the elements that are not visible to your audience but visible to all search engines. Using meta tags is a way of telling the search engines the things that they can expect from your website. Of course, these tags can help your site achieve a higher search engine ranking.

Nowadays, most search engines focus on title, description, and image tags rather than meta tags. However, meta tags are very essential. Since tags are quite difficult to understand, there is a way on how you can appreciate their uses. First, you need to search for a great tool that will enable you to do so. A great tool will help you in maximizing your tags without exerting too much effort. There are opportunities to use the best tools that will help you in maximizing all the tags on your website. Some of these tag tools will help you in finding out all the areas on your website where you can improve your tags in just a few clicks.

Meta Description Tagging mistakes to avoid: A meta description tag is definitely one of the most important elements that your website can have. However, many people fail in understanding how to use it properly and more effectively.

First, you need to understand that when creating a description tag, your primary goal is to tell the search engines what exactly a page contains. You need to do this in an accurate manner if you want to achieve the best results. You should avoid including tags that are not really relevant to your webpage. Some people do "keyword stuffing" in writing their meta description tags. You need to avoid doing that because your website might be penalized or banned by the search engines. Be consistent and specific with your target keywords and do not include the ones that have nothing to do with your website.

Another important thing that you should consider here is the uniqueness of your meta description tag. Spend a few minutes in writing and proofreading it. Do not just copy and paste a part of your website's content. Positive results will only be obtained if you do everything correctly.

URLs: Choosing a good <u>domain name</u> is a very important step, of course. If you think that a domain name is less important than the SEO efforts that you have exerted on your web pages, then you are wrong. A domain name can contribute in your site's search engine rankings. How can you come up with a good domain name? First, recall all the tips that we have discussed earlier about picking the right keywords. Always remember that conciseness is really important when it comes to creating an accurate description. Second, avoid any generalizations and make sure that you are telling the search engines what a webpage contains in a specific way. You need to summarize the content of your page without missing any important point. In other words, your description needs to be short, simple, and meaningful.

Here is a simple example that will help you get an idea on how to come up with a good domain name. Let's say you want to build an affiliate website where you can promote a computer auction site called "computer-auction." You have used Google keyword tools to discover that the keyword "Computer-auction information" can be highly beneficial for your website. If you have decided to use the keyword "Computer-auction tips." That keyword is not bad, but you will surely get much competition if you use that. If that happens, your website might not get a desirable amount of traffic, visitors, and even sales. Of course, your site will also find it extremely difficult to rank in the search engines. You should only choose a domain name that reflects your chosen primary keywords. Of course, you also need to make sure that your website URL reflects your primary keyword.

Domain Analysis: For keyword research, you can use Market Samurai because it allows you to apply some great tricks. If you want to do the same, you may visit http://www.marketsamurai.com/ and buy your own copy of the software. For domain analysis, you can use <u>Alexa</u> and <u>Quantcast</u> because they will allow you to research all relevant links.

Buying Domain Names: <u>Buying Domain names</u> from http://www.goldventureslimited.com will save you more money as the company offers same services for buying all kinds of domain names, website hosting services, and everything else that you can buy from GoDaddy at more affordable cheaper rate. Visit the website link above to check it out.

Content: The key to content is quality and uniqueness. What content should your website's pages contain? Some website owners really find it difficult to come up with great content for every page of their website. It is a bit strange because the content only pertains to what your website offers. So, there is no way for you to get problem with this one. Just focus on your website, particularly to what it offers to your target audience. You should also make sure that your content is unique and of high quality. Search engines ban websites that have copied content, so you need to be extra careful.

The quality and the uniqueness of the content are equally important. However, to make things run smoother and easier, you should first focus on the quality of the content.

The quality of a website's content contributes a lot when it comes to getting more traffic and visitors. If your content is good, your viewers will have good impression of your business. Your content should only focus on what your website wants to say to your readers – nothing more, nothing less. Just focus on your topic and you will do well.

When creating a new content for your website, you should first think of your primary keyword. Next, think of the value of the content to your readers. You need to put yourself into your clients' shoes and provide answers to all the questions that your readers may have in mind while reading your content. If your content focuses on your website's topic and you think that it provides valuable information to your target audience, then you can say that it has high quality.

Now, we will discuss more about the uniqueness of a website. The uniqueness of a website's content will be beneficial to you in 2 ways. First, you will be able to make a content that people cannot find anywhere but on your website only. Your readers would surely love to share it to their friends and contacts. Second, if you create a unique content, you can avoid getting penalties from search engines. In order for you to be motivated in creating unique and high quality content, you need to keep in mind that it will boost the traffic on your website and help generate sales, too.

Links Worth Pursuing: .edu Sites: When working on your website's SEO, you need to pay attention on collecting backlinks because they will help your website in getting a higher rank on the search engine results. However, you always need to keep in mind that the quality is more important than quantity when it comes to building backlinks. In other words, is better to build a backlink on a highly ranked and reputable website than to build 20 or more backlinks from sites that are not reputable and highly ranked.

If you want to build valuable and stable backlinks, you should focus on building links on .edu sites. These sites are highly considered by the search engines. They are also highly ranked most of the time. Here are the things that you need to consider when building backlinks on .edu sites:

If your business focuses on providing products or services for schools or universities, that will give you a huge advantage. If your client has a .edu website, you may ask them if they can add your website URL somewhere on their website and tell their visitors to use your products or services. You also have the choice to contribute some content to .edu sites. You may sponsor events in different schools.

In that way, you will be able to post a link on their website that redirects to your own website.

Finally, you can also apply the old principle of exchanging links. You will post their link on your site and they will post yours in return. It's that simple.

If you have free time, you may read articles on .edu sites and collect some valuable information from them. Once you find something that might appeal to your target audience, then you may write a content that discusses about that topic and do not forget to provide the link to the .edu site where you got that information. That .edu site might just send your website URL to their readers or followers, too.

How to Maximize Your Images: One of the most important keys to success through SEO is learning how to do the things that your competitors fail to do. Believe it or not, your competitors might ignore little things that can contribute to their search engine ranking. You need to know what those little things are and include them in your own SEO strategy. One of the most common things that website builders ignore is using relevant photos on their website.

Tagging your website images properly will contribute a lot on your website's search rankings. Here are the 2 main factors that you should always consider when including images on your site.

The Caption of Your Image: Always add a high quality and SEO-focused description or caption to your image. Use every space to target your primary keyword or a related keyword.

The Text Surrounding Your Image: You should be aware that search engines will use the texts that surround the images on your site. There are 2 ways on how they do it. First, they use the text to determine the relevance of your image to the keyword tag you used. Second, they will use the text to determine the relevance of your keyword tag to the image that you have used. In other words, you need to make sure that your images and the texts around them are relevant to each other. In order words, you need to use your keywords to name and save your images.

The Value of Related Keywords: If you want to achieve success through SEO, you should have 1 or 2 primary keywords for your website. Of course, you need to use those keywords effectively in order for them to be able to contribute in improving your searching engine ranking. Since a primary keyword is considered as the most important factor of a website, people tend to neglect other related keywords that can also generate much traffic on their website.

It might take you some time to get used to integrating or mixing primary and related keywords into a single content in a natural manner, but keep in mind that once you are able to do it correctly, it will go a long way in helping your website to achieve the success that it aims for. The reason it is very ideal to use 2 or more primary keywords is that some people might tend to search using your related keywords instead of the primary one. If you will be able to manage to rank your website for all of your primary and related keywords, then you will double or even triple the chances of generating much traffic on your website.

Some people make mistakes of putting emphasis to their related keywords. It is because they also find it hard to figure out what their related keywords are. If you are also experiencing the same, do not worry. There is one thing that you should be aware of. When it comes to dealing with SEO, you do not really have to work on your own. If you want to expand your website, you may partner with other website owners who can provide you with the right tools that will help you all the way. You might first hesitate to spend money for SEO tools, but you can always make a wise and clever purchase. If you want to get some SEO tools that will help you find related and profitable keywords, diagnose the keywords on your site, and help you in other things that you may not have thought of, you should consider checking out the website links on chapter 7 of this book for these tools. The internet is filled with remarkable tools that will help your website get higher search engine ranking apart from just focusing on the primary and related keywords.

Buyer Keywords: Apart from search engine optimization, you should also focus on targeting your buyers. After all, your main goal in using search engine marketing is to generate sales and make more money. It is great to bring researchers to your website, but it would be better if you will bring more buyers to your website. The best way to target buyers is to learn what the so-called "buyer keywords" are. These keywords are the ones that people are most likely to type in when searching for the products or services that they need and want to buy immediately.

There are two approaches that you can apply when it comes to targeting "buyer keywords." The first approach in targeting buyer keywords is "go it alone" which involves using deductive or logical reasoning to figure out what buyers might want to type into the search engines compared to the ones that researchers type in. This might be a time-consuming task, but once you get used to it, you will surely be able to guess the best keywords that most buyers use in searching for the products that they would like to buy. You are not only a seller, but a customer, too. So, you just need to put yourself into the shoes of other customers. Going it alone and trial and error might not put your website in the highest search engine results, so you need to have another plan. Do you want to achieve high search engine ranking quickly? If so, then you should consider signing up for a membership on a website that will provide you with all the tools that you need to target the best "buyer keywords." I recommend you to use WebFire because it can give you many incredible SEO tools besides their powerful keyword tools. Once you sign up on the site, you will get instant access to the said tools and begin achieving great results immediately. You can consider other websites mentioned on chapter 7.

The Dilemma of Search Engine Ranking with No Converting Sales: If you have already spent much time using SEO to increase your search engine ranking, but you are still not making any money. Is there anything wrong with it? Well, this is indeed a very common problem. You might also experience this especially if you are still a beginner. You do not need to worry about it because there is an easy fix for it. There are 3 main reasons why people visit a search engine site. First, they want to do some academic research. Second, they want to conduct a product research. Third, they want to make a product purchase. If you think that you have done everything to make your site rank high on the search engine results, then there is a big possibility that you were able to target those people who conduct academic and product research. In this case, you just need to change your approach in a way that will focus more on the product purchasers. Believe it or not, it is great news! Many people do not understand this idea, so we can say that you have an edge over your competitors. First, you need to realize that there are several "buyer keywords" that people love to use like "buy…" or "great prices on…" or "best deals on…" Second, you also need to realize that keywords that are composed of multiple words are more likely to be used by customers rather than keywords that are composed of 1 or 2 words only. It is always a great idea to use "long tail keywords". Third, you need to be aware that goggle keyword tool can provide you with so many tools that you can use to guarantee that you are targeting the right keywords that will help you generate sales.

Use of Inbound Links and Content Based Backlinks

Backlinks are definitely important in getting higher search engine ranking for your website. As mentioned before, search engine consider backlinks as "votes of confidence." There are plenty of ways on how to get a huge amount of backlinks for your website. One of the best and most powerful ways to get backlinks is to write articles and submit them to article directories. You might also get paid by those sites by distributing your articles on the Internet. However, this process might be tedious and time-consuming. You should be aware that you will never be allowed to submit an article on different websites because you might get penalized for duplicate content. This simply means that you need to write a unique article for each directory or website that you want to get backlinks from. You may write multiple articles on the same topic, but you need to make sure that each of them is unique.

If you are really serious about building backlinks through article writing, then you should try out 'Free Article Spinner tool or Human Spinner or others. With this awesome tool, you will be able to "spin" your articles to produce unique articles without spending too much effort. Not only that, they can also submit your finished articles to a large number of article directory sites in just a few minutes. What exactly does this mean for online business owners like you? Well, it means that you will have more time to write articles and build as many backlinks as you want! Building backlinks will definitely not only increase your website's success, but also your business' success. You can do this by providing high quality and valuable content and unique information to your visitors that are worth sharing. This is not only the most organic, but also the most productive way to build backlinks. Another great way to get backlinks is to help your readers share your website content easily by putting social media widgets on your website. By doing this, your readers will be able to share your content to their friends and contacts in just a few seconds. Have you ever heard anything about link exchange? Well, you can also use this strategy to get backlinks. This will involve embedding of links to other websites on your web pages. In return, the owners of those websites will also embed your links on their site. Only choose partners that already have high ranked websites. Finally, you may write unique articles and submit them to article directory sites. This process is not just beneficial to your website but also profitable on your part. Those sites will pay you for the content that you have submitted to them. Many article upload tool will help you produce unique articles without spending much time in writing them. You may simply write an article and "spin" it using the tool and you will be able to have unique copies of that article. You may also use the said tool in uploading those articles to article directories in just a few minutes.

Page Ranking and why you need to avoid hard to index pages

You need to make your website very easy for search engines to navigate. You need to be aware that search engines are considered as extremely capable robots that can travel through your site even if you already made everything to make it difficult for them to do so. Search engines can register with ease of navigation on your site.

If your website is not easy to navigate, then search engines will knock it down. Of course, you do not want that to happen, right? The first thing that you need to know when it comes to making your website easy to navigate is that your home page will be the one to get most of the traffic. It is considered as the "root page."

Creating a navigation bar on the side of your website will help it become more user-friendly and easy to navigate. If you do not want to put the bar on the side, you may also choose to put it at the bottom of your site. There is also another way to incorporate this to your site, which is by leaving a so-called "breadcrumb trail."

This is a great way to make your visitors see their own navigation path so that they will be able to return to any of the pages that they have previously visited in a quicker way.

The Difference Between A "site map" and a "Sitemap": A "site map" is the map that your visitors can use to navigate your website easily. On the other hand, a "Sitemap" will never be seen by your visitors. It is created for search engine use only.

Use of Webmaster Tools

Webmaster tools is one of the best free Google tools that you use for SEO. It will help you in achieving the page 1 position that you have always been wanting for your website. One of the most common purposes of Internet marketing is to optimize your website to ensure that it will get many clicks that will bring a huge number of visitors to your website. Webmaster tools can enhance your site and maximize its performance and conversions.

The first thing that you should do once you logged in to Webmaster tool is submit your XML sitemap to the "Sitemap Section" that can be found under "Site Configuration." You may use Google's Webmaster Tools to build & submit a XML Sitemap. You may think that it is just a little thing, but always keep in mind that little things often make big difference and great results on your site's page ranking. The XML sitemap will inform Google that all of your site's URLs need crawling. Once you are done with the submission, it will tell you the total number of pages that you have submitted and it will also inform you how many pages have already been indexed by Google. This tool will help you take action for those pages that have not been indexed by the search engines yet.

Take time to check the "Settings Section" and make sure that your website's geographic target matches your country. Geographical locations can really affect the positioning of your website in the search engine results.

Now, check your results in the Webmaster tools at the "Your Site on the Web" section. You can find all the information regarding the value of your SEO keywords on this page. The search query section on top is a great tool for SEO because it shows all the searches that your website showed up for. It can give you a detailed and comprehensive insight on how many impressions your website has made for every keyword. The results will also show you the number of clicks your site has received through each keyword as well as the "click through rate" (CTR). CTR refers to the percentage of the clicks on your site depending on its position in the search engine results.

Let's say your website is on position 4 and it has an X amount of impressions for a particular keyword. In this case, Webmaster tools will tell you the percentage of the impressions that resulted from the clicks on your site on the search engines.

The "Diagnostics Tab" will enable your website to be checked for Malware or Crawl errors. It will generate all broken links in your website as well as external links that are pointing to a webpage that does not currently exist. These errors can terribly affect your site's SEO, so you need to fix them right away.

In the "Labs" section, you can check your site's performance to see all the important data about your website's page download speed. Google's Webmaster Tools provide information that will help you compare the download speed of your web pages from month to month. This will help you understand if the updates that you have made on a webpage have affected its download speed. Take note that slow download speeds may lower your search engine ranking.

The data will also tell you whether your site's download speed is faster or slower than that of your competitors.

Using Google's Webmaster Tool is an effective way to take control over your website. It will help you get your site exposed on the search engines. It will also help you in analyzing your website and learn how to make it get a better performance. It will also let you know if there were errors that Google has encountered while crawling your site. In other words, it will help you in debugging your site. It can also notify you if there are HTTP errors on your website. It will allow you to submit your website for reconsideration if in case it was already banned by Google for some reason.

Search Engine Listing Status

Do you want to let the search engines know that you have just built a new website or if you have just posted a new content on your site? That is not a problem then! Just take a few seconds to fill the form and hit "Submit." It will help you alert all top sites. This will help you increase your chances of getting your website indexed on search engines and reach higher ranking.

Don't Forget Social Media Is Part Of SEO: When you are working on the SEO of your site, you should never ever ignore some small things that will contribute to your website's success. One of the most powerful factors that will help your website obtain huge amount of traffic and high search engine ranking is social media! You can easily build backlinks through social media.

Another reason why social media is a very important factor for SEO is that it can help you to get many visitors for your site.

Here are the things that you need to do to make sure that you are able to maximize the impact of your website through social media.

First, you need to make it easy for your visitors to share the content of your website through social media. You may add widgets to your website's pages so your visitors will be able to share any content that catches their attention in just a click!

Second, pay attention to social media sharing. You may do this by adding "Share" widgets with your website's content.

Lastly, you need to put efforts in creating a social media presence for your business. You may create a Twitter account, a Facebook page, a Pinterest account, or even a Google Plus account.

Never ever forget to use social media on your SEO projects and always use it well!

Search Engine Marketing (SEM)

The first step in successful Search engine marketing is attracting visitors. Search engine marketing is indeed a great way to make money from your website. However, you should be aware that even though many people have been successful in this field, there are more people who failed to make their website get higher ranking. Before thinking of any advanced method about search engine marketing, you should always remember its basic concept which is to get visitors to your website. You need to understand that search engine optimization (SEO) is a multilayered process that is divided into 3 primary keys which include keywords, backlinks, and meta tags. Once you have learned the importance of each of those key factors, the next thing that you should do is search for the perfect tool that will help you get the most out of your SEO efforts. You may sign up for a membership on the relevant websites listed on chapter 7 of this book to get instant access to all the amazing tools that they offer. Making money through search engine marketing is really easy. You just need to have basic knowledge of SEO and a tool that will help you in saving time with SEO tasks.

What Content Your SEM Articles Should Contain: As you study search engine optimization, you will surely understand that article writing is one of the best ways to boost the traffic of your website. Do not get too excited about it because you should first decide the things that your articles should discuss. Do not worry. Article writing is not really tough. You just need to spend enough time for it.

Before starting to write any article, you should first understand that it needs to be relevant to the content of your website. You should not make a mistake in doing this because misleading articles might greatly affect your business. You need to know what exactly to do before taking any action. Do not just write articles. Make them meaningful and useful for your target audience. Include the right amount of keywords and backlinks to your article, too. Always keep in mind that your readers will read your articles. They will not just click the backlinks that you have included in them. They will only click your links and visit your website if they think that your articles are interesting and beneficial to them. Your content should also be engaging so that they will never think twice in visiting your website.

If you need help in writing articles, then you can get it immediately. You can cut your time in writing engaging articles by simply using the article uploader tools. When you visit the relevant links on chapter 7 of this book, you will get access to some of the best SEO tools including article spinner and uploader tools that will help you produce multiple articles and submit them immediately to article directories.

Monitoring your Competitors

Market research is considered as a crucial starting process that any business should always undergo. You need to find a profitable niche and analyze your competitors on that niche. Market research requires much time, so you need to plan in order for you to do it successfully. You can look for target customers that are willing to buy your products even before you launch them in the market. Always consider to use the Internet when it comes to performing market research. There are so many affordable or even free marketing tools that you can get from the Internet. When it comes to doing market research for an online business, you do not need to target customers by geographic location. You just need to find people who share similar interest.

Market research can be done on the web, through electronic mail, and by using newsgroups. The Internet will perfectly help you when it comes to checking your competitors and researching for the most profitable niche. Why do you need to research your competition? First, you need to know the number of businesses who sell the same product as yours. More companies that sell similar products would mean tougher competition. Researching for your competition will also help you in focusing more on your business and working hard for it. You will also learn a lot from competition research. You may learn some strategies that your competitors have not used yet. It will give you an edge over your rivals. In any competition, it is very important for you to "know your enemy." Find out how your competitors sell their products. Do not forget to check out their pricing as well as their marketing campaigns. Think competitively and always keep an eye on your competitors. Once you are done with the competition research, you should create a simple survey that contains all the questions about your competitors' businesses. Who will be the participants of your survey? Well, you can do it both online and offline. If you already have a website, you may simply post the form there. You may also post your survey on newsgroups. You may also send it through e-mail. As you can see, there are really many ways on how to get the opinion of your target audience.

Just ask some people, ideally your target audience, to fill out your survey form. Once they are done, do your analysis right away.

You may also use free classified pages online to get survey participants. Some people do not like to give a favor without something in return. So, you may offer them discount codes, coupons, or freebies so that they will be motivated to fill out your survey.

Google can also help you when it comes to online market research. During your spare time, investigate the most popular keywords or the keywords that obtain many searches online. You may also check out the latest trends in the industry where you belong. In that way, you will get an idea about the things that your target audience would like to buy.

Free Google Tools for Online business

Here I have discussed about key 12 Free Google Tools for your online Business. I want to help you in getting the right tools for your online business without the need to spend much money.

Here is the list of my Top 12 Free Google Tools for Starting your online Businesses or growing your online business:

Blogger: Blogging is an ideal way to show your expertise to your target audience. Google has a free blogging service that you can use to write weblogs and share them to your readers. It is called "Blogger." If you want to make some money by blogging, it would be recommended for you to migrate your blogger site to your website's subdomain. Example: blog.youdomain.com

YouTube Channel: If you want to try out video marketing, then you should have your own YouTube Channel. This channel will keep all of your tutorials, promotions, events, skits, or video blogs. You may even organize them accordingly. YouTube also allows you to embed your videos to your website, blog, Facebook page, Twitter page, or anywhere that can read the embed codes of YouTube videos.

Picasa – Picasa is a picture editor and album. Google's Picasa allows you to put all of your corporate pictures in one place. You can also grab the HTML code for each image and embed them either on your site or on your social media pages.

Google Places: Contains local search or maps listing. Google Places offer a free listing on Google maps. This will help your customers in tracking where your business or office is located. You can optimize it by embedding suitable keywords, images, map, and content. You may also embed discount coupons on it.

Gmail: If you love Gmail for personal use, you will also love it for business use. You can setup a Gmail account for your startup business easily and quickly. You need to have a professional e-mail address, so you need to set it up through your own domain. Example: info@yourdomain.com

Google Voice: If you want to get a phone number by your area code or business name, you should check out Google Voice. You can use it to setup a custom number that will redirect your customers' calls to your landline or mobile phone. Not only that. You will also get an e-mail or text transcript of your voicemail. You may either listen to it or read it whenever you want to.

Online Calendar: Google's Online Calendar will help you become updated with your schedules. You can share it with your friends, too. You may even synchronize it with your mobile phone or other electronic devices conveniently.

Use it to send event invitations or to track all RSVPs. It is very recommended if you already have employees.

Google Docs: Is an Online document sharing tool. Google Docs is an awesome sharing system. You can upload documents and share it to your staff and colleagues. You can use this to keep your documents updated. Many businesses use this for lead generation, sharing reports, and recording bills.

Google Alerts: It sends you latest updates for any topic. Google Alerts are e-mail updates on the latest trends for any topic of your choice. You can use them to track the latest updates about your market.

Behind the Scene Google Tools

Webmaster Tools: Google's Webmaster Tools can help you in improving your website's performance.

Google Keyword Tool: Google Adwords Keyword Tool can help you in finding the local and global monthly searches, competition, and latest trends for a specific keyword. You can use this for keyword and competition research.

Google Analytics: Google Analytics is a tool that will help you track down everything that is happening on your website. You can use this to see the traffic statistics of your website as well as the information of every visitor that visits your site.

By using all of these 12 tools, you will not only save money but also make greater improvements to your business. These tools will help you in organizing your business stuff.

Check out these other Google tools/Networks for generating more revenue:

- <u>Google Adwords</u>
- <u>Google Adsense Plugin for WordPress</u>
- <u>Google App engine</u>
- <u>Google DoubleClick</u>
- <u>Google Affiliate Network</u>
- <u>Google Partner programs</u>
- <u>Google Adsense</u>
- <u>Google Engage</u>
- <u>Google+ for Business</u>
- <u>Google Apps for Business</u> etc

Chapter 6
Now to Make It All Legal

In This Chapter

Making Copyright Work for You

Staying Out of Legal Trouble

Understanding Legal Basics

Consumer Protection Regulations

Keeping Record of Business Transactions

Appointing an Accountant or Using Accounting Software

Copywriting

Making Copyright Work for You

You need to be aware of the online copyright services that have been installed on the Internet that prevents people from commit plagiarism. If you want to pass the plagiarism checks online, you need to ensure that you content is 100% unique and meaningful. Content that was copied from other sources are not tolerated on the Internet. Never ever use copied content if you do not want your website to get penalized.

If your business offers or deals with intellectual properties, you really need to use copyright services. You need to secure or protect your own unique content so that other websites that offer the same services will not be able to copy it. If you want to make money online, you should do your best to avoid having negative effect your business and your customers. To avoid this, you should only hire a reliable copyright service provider that can protect your website and all of its contents online if you desire to do so.

Staying Out of Legal Trouble

To stay out of legal trouble, you need to check and comply with all legal requirements first. In the UK, you need to register your business name with the <u>Companies House</u>. In the US, you need to register your business and get your Tax ID number for your business. You may visit <u>IRS.gov</u> to register a Tax ID number. This number can be used in place of your SSN. You will get your ID number in just a couple of days. You can also register with your respective country by searching for your country's business registration department.

Once you have already obtained a Tax ID number, you need to secure a resale card or a seller's permit. This will allow you to buy all the items that you want to sell without paying taxes. All taxes will be paid by your end users every time they buy your items.

When running an online business, you may also want to file your taxes as a sole proprietor, LLC etc (instead of self-employed). As a sole proprietor or LLC etc, you will get many benefits like tax breaks, <u>deducting business expenses</u> etc whenever you send your personal income. For UK, you can check out <u>Gov.uk</u> .

The last thing that you need to get is your business license or business registration. Yes, you need this even though you are just operating an online business. You may just need to visit the relevant website for your state, country or location to check the exact specifications and requirements.

If you want to ensure the safety of your business, you need to take a number of steps that will keep your online business running for a very long time without facing any legal issues.

Trademark Registration: This will help you in putting all of your products, logos, packaging, and ideas secured on the Internet. If you can afford it, do it.

Protect Your Hardware and Software: Hackers are everywhere. They want to access all of your confidential information, so you need to prevent them from affecting your website and other online business accounts. You need to make sure that all of your financial and other confidential records are safe and well-protected.

Keep Your Domain Name Protected: There is nothing wrong with buying only one domain name. However, it would be much better if you will buy domain names that contain the spelling variations of your current domain name.

Make Sure Your Forums Are Safe and Private: If you are currently running a forum, you always need to keep it secured. Keep in mind that you are responsible for any crime that will occur on your forum site, so you need to make sure that all personal information are secured by using security software.

Understanding Legal Basics

Here are some of the most important details that startup business owners should understand.

Sole-Proprietorship: This is the most typical business setup. It means that only you own the business. All obligations and properties come from you.

Partnership: This means that a business is run or administered by 2 or more people. Business partners will share all the gains, losses, or even debts all the time.

Corporation, Limited Company or Limited Liability Company (LCC): It has an advanced structure. It is recognized by the law and it has the same obligations and privileges of a person. This type of business needs to pay taxes and complexities. There is a double taxation issue in this kind of business. Double taxation means that the business owner will need to pay the taxes on the gains that the business generates as well as the income that he gets as an individual. The company will also need to make an annual tax return and pay an annual tax on the total shares.

S Corporation: It is similar to LLC, but it does not involve double taxation. The Internal Revenue Service (IRS) allows this type of business to be taxed as a partnership and not as a corporation. In order for your business to have an S status, it needs to comply with 3 conditions that the IRS requires: (1) small group and shareholders in the business; (2) limited stock issued reasonably; (3) regulated sources of profit. These structures have surely given you an understanding of the type of concept that suits your business better.

Licenses and Contracts: Never ever sign a contract or agreement without reading it. Everybody knows this, but still, some people ignore reading huge chunk of texts that are printed in an agreement form. If you are not sure of whatever that is written on a certain contract or agreement, you should contact your lawyer and ask for his or her advice.

It is also beneficial to learn more about the Internet laws. There are lawyers that specialize in this subject so you may just hire one to assist you if you want.

The Internet law involves problems with intellectual properties as well as any legal issues that deal with trademark contravention and transgression, domain name licensing, cybersquatting etc

Cybersquatting refers to the illegal registration or use of a domain name that is based on a registered trademark.

Consumer Protection Regulations

The primary aim of the Consumer Protection Law is to protect consumer rights and welfare from exploitation of the marketers and traders. It also aims to provide honest and reliable information in the marketplace. Some consumers are not aware of the marketing information so they just tend to buy items without complete knowledge about its quality and cost. There are cases when products are found to be contaminated and can harm the health or lives of the consumers. These are the main reasons why the consumer protection law should always be given much importance. You should always be extra careful when choosing the items that you are going to buy. Some traders deceive their customers by providing them misleading information about the real origin of their products. Always beware of scammers and only deal with legitimate traders that already have proven track record. Scammers are everywhere, so you should always do your best to get rid of them. If you want to get some effective tips on how to recognize scammers or scam businesses, you may simply seek the help of the Office of Fair Trading (OFT). They always offer a list of the latest types of scams.

The Consumer Protection Law gives you the right to complain to any company or trader that had sold inadequate goods to you. It is also possible for you to hire an experienced and knowledgeable solicitor who can work on your behalf. The said solicitor will also give you some advice and guide that will help you in handling your case.

In case the company that you have sued was not able to respond on your allegation, the Director-General of Fair Trade will be the one to deal with the Consumer Protection issues.

Keeping Record of Business Transactions

Your business needs professional account management as it grows. You have 2 options for this. First, you may hire an in-house professional. Second, you may outsource the job to companies that are offering small business bookkeeping services. Most companies recruit professionals to invest reasonable amount of time, effort, and money in their recruitment, training, and adaptation with the company's processes and culture. Because of this, their focus might shift from their core business activities which may lead to loss of customers and sales.

Advantages of Small Business Bookkeeping Services

A professional can record complicated financial transactions like sales, purchases, payments, and receipts. All of these transactions should be recorded into the general ledger, customer ledger, correct day book, and supplies ledger. This task may seem to be simple and straightforward, but it is not. This job will require accuracy in filling in the correct data. No decimal should be recorded incorrectly. Everything should be precise and accurate. Only trained professionals should be assigned to this type of task. However, make sure you do the correct thing. Small business accounting service providers always employ the best accountants in the industry to do book keeping and accounting tasks for their clients. These service providers perform better than the in-house book keeping professionals most of the time. Small business bookkeeping services are usually cheaper than the service charges of in-house book keeping professionals. Since insurance and gratuity are not involved in this case, business owners will surely get exceptional services that cost less than the salary of a full-time employee. Small business bookkeeping service providers can take good care of the security measures, too. They will ensure that all unauthorized individuals will not get access to the confidential files of the company. They will also make sure that all sensitive information will be password-protected all the time.

Appointing an Accountant or Using Accounting Software

Some small business owners collaborate with online business accounting firms. These firms are responsible for tracking down their daily records, sales, and expenses. They also take good care of the accounting books of different firms. These firms usually offer service packages that include tax planning, bookkeeping, and balance sheet information. They also settle the companies' bank accounts every month. They will ensure that every bank reconciliation statement is accurate and free from any type of errors. They will also correct any mistake in the banking transactions so that the business owners will never get any problem. Whether you are a businessperson or a retired person, you can use bookkeeping services for any of your financial guides like personal tax returns, small business taxes, or corporate tax returns. If you are interested in using accounting software, you need to understand that it will require you some money, time, and effort in order for it to work successfully. You need to put close attention to it in order for you to yield higher return on investment (ROI) quickly.

The Benefits of Accounting Software for Businesses: Accounting software is used to speed up all accounting processes. This software also has the ability to protect the financial details of a company. Not only that, it can also help in maintaining the accuracy of all information that has been inputted in the system. In order for you to get bigger benefits from your accounting software, you need to consider the following tips:

Decide Which Software Features are Required by the Business: Before getting accounting software for your company, you should first check if its specifications are perfectly suited to your business requirements.

Find an Industry-Specific Software for the Business: Some accounting applications are industry-specific. It would be ideal to get one that matches to the industry where your business belongs.

Check for Free Trial Versions: It is always good to take advantage of the free trial version of accounting software. By using the free trial version, you will be able to use the program before paying for it. It will help you decide better if you can really use that application to your business' accounting processes.

Customization: Some companies that create accounting applications offer software customization. They will customize the system based on your company's needs and specifications. Some accounting applications are generic, so they need to be customized in order for you to be able to use them in your company.

Invest on a Good Accounting Software: As a business owner, you are surely looking for a high ROI (Return On Investment). In order for you to obtain the ROI that you desire for your business, you should invest in a reliable, and highly functional, accounting software.

Copywriting

Copywriting refers to the process of writing content that conveys promotional message to its readers. Believe it or not, an effective copy plays a very important role in generating sales for your business. In this case, you need to write persuasive content that will persuade your target audience to buy your products. A copywriter is responsible for the copywriting task. The output that he or she delivers is called "copy." A copy can be a long piece of content that is intended for sales letters and websites. There are also copies that are really short, just like the ones that you read on newspapers or phonebook advertisements. You can hire a copywriter to create a great sales copy for you. However, if you do not want to spend money to pay for a copywriting service, you may simply create your own sales copy. Here are some of the best copywriting tips that will help you in writing an effective sales copy.

Make Use Of The Internet: You can find learning materials that will help you develop your copywriting skills online. Some of them can be downloaded for free.

Keep Ideas Simple: If you want to get the interest of your readers, you should avoid using complex words. Be as simple and specific as possible.

Get To Know Your Audience: You need to know who your target audience is before writing a copy. You need to learn how to communicate with them very well. You also need to know how your audience feels and thinks about the product that you are promoting to them.

Be Creative, Be Unique: Uniqueness and creativity is very important in copywriting. Your readers should be able to learn something from your copy so that they will be interested in trying out the product that you are promoting. Of course, you should not use sentences that may sound boring to them. Use lines that will amuse or entertain them while reading your entire copy.

Chapter 7
Do You know About These Great Websites?

<u>In This Chapter</u>

Domain, Web Hosting, Web Designing, etc

Domain & Hosting Reseller Website

Affiliate Marketing Websites

Best Online Forums

Where to Find Online Skills Jobs

Social Media Networking Sites

Search Engine Optimization & Ranking Tools.

Leads Generation Websites

Customer Relations Management (CRM) Websites

Article Marketing Websites

Online Advertising Websites, etc

A list of many websites has been included here with different categories to help guide you towards finding what you need in making your online business a success. That these websites have been included here does not mean endorsement of the websites. However, careful research has been done to ensure that you are offered the best information that is available. Most of these websites are underground websites used by internet millionaires. If you can check them out and apply most of the strategies offered including the ones discussed about in this book, there is no way you cannot become an internet millionaire before the next 5 years.

Domain, Web Hosting, Web Designing etc

Gold Ventures Domain & Hosting

http://www.goldventureslimited.com

http://www.goldventuresdomainandhosting.com

GoDaddy.com

http://www.godaddy.com/?isc=iapwd30a

Domain & Hosting Reseller Website

Domain & Hosting Reseller Business

http://www.goldventureslimited.co.uk

Affiliate Marketing

http://www.clickbank.com

http://www.offervault.com

http://www.clicksure.com

http://www.commission-junction.com

http://www.cj.com/

http://www.linkshare.com/

http://www.shareasale.com

http://affiliate-program.amazon.com

http://www.clixgalore.com

http://www.peerfly.com

http://www.maxbounty.com/

http://www.neverblue.com

http://www.clickbooth.com

Online Forums

http://www.warriorforum.com

http://www.emillionforum.com

http://forums.digitalpoint.com

http://partner.linkedin.com/influencer

http://www.craiglist.com/

http://forums.craiglist.org

Where to find Online skills job

http://www.elance.com

http://www.fiverr.com

http://www.odesk.com

http://www.guru.com

http://www.freelance.com

http://www.peopleperhour.com

♦ Website building tools

DreamWeaver CS6

http://www.adobe.com/uk/products/dreamweaver.html

Social Media Networking

http://www.mashable.com

http://www.twitter.com/

http://www.facebook.com

http://www.pinterest.com

http://www.slideshare.net

http://plus.google.com

http://www.linkedin.com

http://www.justretweet.com

http://www.myspace.com

http://www.stumbleupon.com

http://www.reddit.com

Search Engine Optimization & Ranking tools

http://www.keywordspy.com

http://www.alexa.com

http://www.webfire.com

http://www.google.com/webmaster

http://www.seoquake.com

http://www.semrush.com

http://www.whorush.com

http://www.searchenginejournal.com

http://www.monitorbacklinks.com

http://www.linkdiagnosis.com

http://www.pingomatic.com

https://freekeywords.wordtracker.com/

http://www.compete.com/

http://www.prchecker.info/

http://www.seoprofiler.com

http://www.seomoz.org/

Leads Generation

http://www.getsubscribers.com

http://www.craiglist.org/

Customer Relations Management (CRM) Systems

http://www.aweber.com/?413146

http://www.aweber.com/?413146

http://www.infusionsoft.com

http://www.mouseflow.com

http://www.trafficwave.com

- ♦ Keywords and Link Building

http://www.statcounter.com/

http://www.marketsumarai.com

http://www.officeautopilot.com

http://www.wordtracker.com

http://www.wordtracker.com/linkbuilder

http://freekeywords.wordtracker.com

Article marketing

99Centarticles

http://www.1shoppingcart.com/app/?af=1516281

http://www.ezinearticles.com

http://www.goarticles.com/

http://www.articlebase.com

http://www.articlealley.com

http://www.articlemarketer.com

http://www.articledashboard.com

http://www.isnare.com

http://www.buzzle.com

http://www.articlecity.com

http://www.upublish.info

http://www.site-reference.com

http://www.amazines.com

- ◆ Expedited article submission

http://www.submitedge.com

Online Marketing websites

http://www.ebay.com

http://www.ebay.co.uk

http://www.amazon.com

http://www.traffiq.com

http://www.valueclick.com/

http://www.zedo.com

http://www.valueclickmedia.com

http://www.trafficvance.com

- ◆ Mind mapping tools

http://www.mindjet.com

♦ Online Business Book website

http://www.thesecretcodetosuccessandwealth.com

♦ Prototyping Tools

http://www.keynotopia.com

♦ Article Spinner

http://www.humanspinner.com

http://www.ezarticlelink.com/articlespinner/free.php

http://www.webfire.com/a/?id=2614

Spin Rewriter

http://www.spinrewriter.com/?ref+ad1b

♦ Video creation software with free trial

http://www.techsmith.com - Camtasia

♦ Tracking Tools

Tracking 202

http://www.tracking202.com

Tracking202

http://prosper.tracking202.com

♦ Keywords research

Market Samurai

http://www.marketsamurai.com

♦ Keyword Spy

http://www.keywordspy.com

♦ Blogging

Google Blogger

http://www.blogger.com

http://www.wordpress.org

http://www.squidoo.com

http://www.copyblogger.com

http://www.problogger.net

- ♦ URL Rotator Script

http://www.ljscripts.com/freescripts

http://www.codecanyon.net

- ♦ Google Tools

Google placement Targeting

Google Content Network

Content bids

Placement-targeted ads

Google Placement tool

Content Bully

Google Network

Google Affiliate Network

- ♦ PPC/CPC Platforms

http://www.mediatrust.com

http://www.pulse360.com

http://www.adblade.com

http://www.adonnetowrk.com

http://advertising.aol.com

http://www.advertising.com

http://www.clicksor.com

♦ Other PPC platforms

http://www.usatoday.com

http://www.snagajob.com

http://www.weather.com

♦ Domain Analysis

http://www.alexa.com

http://www.quantcast.com

http://www.compete.com

♦ Hot Trends

eBay Pulse

http://pulse.ebay.com

Google Trends

http://www.google.com/trends

http://www.google.co.uk/trends/hottrends

http://www.google.com/trends/hottrends

♦ Affiliate Tracking Software

http://www.hasoffers.com

http://www.tracking202.com

http://www.idevdirect.com

http://www.directtrack.com

http://www.postaffiliatepro.com

http://www.affiliateroyale.com

http://www.clickinc.com

Prosper202

http://prosper.tracking202.com/apps

- ◆ PPV/CPV Network

http://www.directcpv.com

http://www.trafficvance.com

http://www.mediatraffic.com

http://www.affexpert.com

- ◆ Traffic Systems you can use

Article Traffic

Facebook traffic

Blog traffic

Search traffic

Solo ad traffic

PR traffic

Video traffic

Twitter traffic

Web 2.0 traffic

Affiliate Traffic

Google Traffic

- ◆ Facebook Advertising

http://www.facebook.com/advertising

- ◆ Amazon web services

aws.amazon.com

- ◆ CPA Networks

http://www.affiliateseeking.com

Over 140 CPA networks

http://www.clickbooth.com

http://www.neverblue.com

http://www.maxbounty.com/

http://PeerFly.com

http://www.mediawhiz.com/

http://www.cpaway.com/

http://www.adscendmedia.com/

http://www.convert2media.com

http://www.w4.com/

http://www.adknowledge.com/

http://www.cpalead.com/

http://www.matomymarket.com/

http://www.intela.com

http://www.revenuestreet.com/

http://www.adworkmedia.com/

http://www.fluentco.com/

http://www.xRevMedia.com/

http://www.motiveinteractive.com/

http://www.valuleads.com

http://www.ads4dough.net/

http://www.paydotcom.com

- ◆ Backlinking

http://www.dropmylink.com

Read Unlimited Free Ebooks

Read Unlimited Free Ebooks

http://goo.gl/zqzSY

- ♦ Search Engines

http://www.pingomatic.com/

- ♦ Miscellaneous

http://www.webpronews.com

- ♦ Online Classified Ads sites

http://www.craigslist.com

http://www.oodle.com

http://www.livedeal.com

http://www.hoobly.com

http://www.backpage.com

http://www.myspace.com/classifiedads

http://www.srds.com

http://jaysonbenoit.com/solo_ads/

- ♦ Social plugins

http://www.addthis.com

- ♦ Offline advertising

Newspaper classified listings

Networking meetings

Business events etc

- ♦ Great Business Apps for phones

Bizplan by Docstoc Inc

Facebook pages manager

Samcard – Professional business card reader

- ♦ Business Grant funding UK

http://www.bis.gov.uk

http://www.grantfinder.co.uk

http://www.fundingcentral.org.uk

http://www.j4bgrants.co.uk

- ♦ US Business Grants

http://www.grants.gov

http://business.usa.gov/

http://www.usa.gov/

- ♦ EU Business Grants

http://www.access2finance.eu

- ♦ Business/Project funding websites

http://www.kickstarter.com

- ♦ Business Networks

http://www.weetu.org

http://www.businesslink.gov.uk

http://www.startupbritain.org

http://www.startups.co.uk

- ♦ Business Plan Websites

http://www.bplans.com/

http://www.bplans.co.uk

Chapter 8
Getting the Latest Tools and Strategies to Help You

In This Chapter

Leads and Traffic Generation Strategies

Use of Google Adwords, Google Adsense, Google Analytics, Page Speed, YouTube Partners

SEO & Link Building

Article Marketing, Spinning and Blogging

List Building

Online Auctions

CPA Networks

Benefits of Using Advertising Options like Media Buying, PPV, CPC, CPL Traffic, Banner Advertising, CPM, CPA etc

Use of Social Media (Facebook, Twitter, LinkedIn, YouTube, Slide share, Pinterest My Space)

Social Bookmarking and Creating Product Review Website

Email Ad's & Marketing Strategies

Use of Affiliate Marketing Websites

Leads and Traffic Generation Strategies

Finding leads that are effective is one of the most important things for growing your sales and overall success of your business. After all, finding leads that do work for one's business could be burdensome and time consuming but it's just a typical situation. Though this seems frustrating, there is still good news for you to be encouraged towards searching for leads that could work better for your business. In addition, keeping both your particulars and your leads which are proven effective can let you gain some edge over your competitors. However, it is important for you to be always diligent and not immediately buy such leads. First, you should remember that it is not all lead generators and database that are created equally. Thus, you have to find out how these leads were collected and examine others' experience with similar leads from the same provider. This will help you evaluate whether the investment that you are about to make is going to be a success. It is also important to know if it is worth spending a bit of extra money on leads or not. Always remember that leads are not automatically converting leads because they are bought at high cost.

Financially, when you buy leads, it allows you to generate traffic volume. However, you should also realize that the leads you generate can probably and often are the most valuable leads of all. This is because you are certain that the people you will be contacting are interested in your business more specifically compared to those you contacted through the leads you bought. It is possible to collect leads of your own by setting up your website and other campaigns of your business. After that, you will be able to turn these leads into large volume of sales. Finally, always remember that the result of your leads depends on the manner of your approach. If you feel that all your leads turned out to be failures, try to look back because there might be something you need to adjust. Study how to turn your leads into cash. Through this, you will find out if leads can bring you to success.

How to Turn Leads into Sales: Most business owners spend much time trying to figure out how to buy the best leads as possible. However, what they all need to realize is that what you call "best leads" are simply the leads which turn into sales. After all, one thing is for sure – a poor salesperson can lose even the best of leads but a great salesperson can turn even the coldest of leads into red hot sales. Thus, everything still depends upon you as a salesperson. There are three things you will need to keep in mind to turn your leads into sales.

Keep the Goal in Mind: The primary goal of every lead is to turn it into a customer. Do not be fooled with numbers and statistics about the pursuit of these leads because you always have to remember that your primary concern here is to deal with your customers. However, you do not have to assume that all your ten leads will be converted into ten customers. Otherwise, you might gain zero. On the other hand, if you start focusing at one lead at a time, you are likely to end up being successful repeatedly.

Make an Impact: If you are following a lead, there is always a great chance that there are others who are following the same lead as yours. Thus, you have to make a create an impression to make the sale. Be quick when contacting the leads, interact with them personally and make everything clear and understandable. If you do these simple things, you will be a step away from other persons who are following the same lead at the same time as you.

Keep the Basics as Your Foundation: You will need to get back to your clients to interact with them, asking relevant questions and answering them thoroughly. Do this in a professional and a respectful manner. However, do not forget to research so you are able to explain and explore about any topic people may ask you. Instead, just stick to the basics about good business. Through this, you will automatically increase your return by turning leads into sales.

Internet, business and profit are 3 important words. Integrating all them into a successful venture will require you to have another important word – Traffic. If you try to research about making your site successful, you will find in every article that they would always include the importance of generating traffic. Thus, we can generalize that the core of it all is traffic. It is the most essential thing for an internet based company to be successful. That is why you have to ensure that apart from having great products to sell and having a well company, you should also prioritize generation of traffic.

However, if you already have a site but you are not getting the traffic that you should be getting, then it's time for you to get things done. Contending with a competitive business will require you to step ahead of your competitors. Remember, increasing your traffic flow should have been done earlier than sooner. Another important thing to consider is timing. It is very essential that you must keep it in mind. However, when generating traffic, you should always be vigilant and always be ahead of competition. Always think that yesterday should have been the starting point of driving traffic into your site. Never think about today and tomorrow as your starting point. To help you in generating more traffic, here are 7 ways to increase your converting traffic:

Invest in Good Advertising with Search Engines: To get great advertising campaign which are very popular and can assure quality traffic, Google Adwords and Yahoo Overture are two of the top names. These two can certainly increase your traffic; however, they would cost some money. While you would hesitate to spend money for it, it is still worth considering that Adwords and Overture are the best ways to increase your website traffic. As you will observe, these search engine advertising methods have brought success and reaped rewards for so many companies. Lots of sites feature this advertising system and many have signed on to take advantage of the benefits. It is good not to be left behind. Always remember that with Google and Yahoo's advertising, every penny you spend is worth it.

Exchange or Trade Links with Other Sites: Exchanging links with other sites will benefit both parties especially in generating traffic. When the first site generates another site's link, the second site could get the traffic the first site generates. The efforts are beneficial because both of you are doing something to drive more traffic. The more links you trade, the more traffic you can expect.

Use Viral Marketing: Viral marketing is a process of spreading information about what your company and product is all about without any cost or if any, with minimal fee. However, this marketing method can be quite interesting. This is done by attaching your company's name, product or link to a certain media. Your platform can be in a form of a funny video, entertaining game or an interesting article or a gossip or buzz. By using this method, people get curious about the creativity and entertainment the medium brings and will likely share it to other people.

Search and Use Correct Keywords or Keyword Phrases for Your Site's Content: Certain keywords are what search engines search for to show in their result page. To do this, you need the correct keyword as it will also help you obtain a high ranking in search engines. Moreover, in writing content, some would hire article experts but if you have the inclination for writing, you certainly can do it on your own.

Write Articles That Can Lead Traffic to Your Site: Write articles and submit them to sites which contain similar subject to yours. For example, if you are selling car parts, you can write press releases and articles about cars and car parts. Then, finish your contents by attaching your site's description, services and link.

Join Forums and Form Online Communities: Showing your expertise and credibility can be done by attracting your target market. People will trust you when you are able to build a good foundation for your site. Through this, your traffic will increase so is your profit.

Offer Newsletters: Through recommendation from your loyal readers, more traffic will be generated to your site. However, this will only happen if you could stir your customers' curiosity. In that way, people will know what you business or site is about. After that, your existence will be shared by these people to many others. These are strategies you can use to generate traffic using free methods:

Trends Traffic: When doing online marketing, following perfect trends makes sense to everyone. Do you know that eBay can be used to identify what is hot on the market and pages? Yes! By using eBay Pulse, you can see the hottest categories on eBay. Another place where you can follow the trends is in Google Trends. Google Trends allow you to see websites that are listed by Google according to particular keywords as well as trends that you can follow.

We all know that starting a company would obviously require lots of important things like, you need money or capital. Every business owner knows that to earn money requires money as well. However, because of these versatilities that the internet offers, there are so many avenues you could use to help you optimize the potential of your website or business to generate traffic.

Obviously, it is very much desirable to have more traffic to your site by literally spending nothing. There are available sites over the internet offering free articles with tips and guidelines on how to increase traffic by using free methods. This is because of the possibility to drive traffic while spending nothing, though it may take time. However, paying for ads will take you shorter time but at least, there is still that opportunity of obtaining this for free and this is what we will be exploring.

Capitalize on online communities & online forums: Online forums and online communities are amazing because they allow you to target a certain group that fits the certain demographic or particular group of persons that you are looking for. Through this, it also allows you to discuss many important details about a certain niche that you represent or offer. In addition, you have the advantage because you already know what you are getting and you are prepared for it. By joining online communities and forums, it helps you to earn reputation for yourself and your company. You can build reputation and earn their trust by showing them what you are made of and impress them with your range of expertise about the subject.

Use of Newsletters: Making newsletters is also an effective method. You can provide people with catalogs of your products and articles which are interesting and entertaining. The more they are interesting and entertaining, the more people will sign up for your newsletter and they will recommend it to their friends. If this happens, the visitors you will get for your site will certainly increase leading to excellent traffic.

Trading Links: Trading links with other sites is also a great idea. This method will not cost you any cent or pence. This can be simply done by having an agreement with other websites. By exchanging links, both sites will benefit from each other's effort. The visitors of the first site could potentially click on the link of the other site and visit the second site as well. This process is effective especially if both sites feature the same niche.

Article Writing: Another simple way is to write articles that could attract the attention of people who have interest in your product. Writing articles that provide tips and guides to other people can also help. Articles that provide good service and information to the people would provide the necessary advantage of increasing your traffic flow. Post articles on sites offering free submission and posting. If people become interested in your articles, there is a good chance that they might follow the track to find out where the article originally came from. You should include a brief description and a link to your online business in the article. This will give you a greater chance of increasing your traffic.

Writing Good Content for Your Website: Another important thing is that you should write a good content for your website. The keywords and keyword phrases your site uses and how they are used are what search engines look for. You do not have to be a professional writer to do this. You just need to make sure that your site contains entertaining and informative content. It should maintain the standard requirements as well as have an excellent quality.

Generally, search engines provide their users what they are searching for. In return, search engines use keywords to facilitate their search results. Thus, you should use the right keywords to get high rankings without spending too much. All of these methods and more will help your website to drive more traffic for free. All you just need is a bit of effort and extended time. Just learn and apply the methods discussed here and soon, your site will have a great traffic flow without spending the usual cost most people pay.

Use of Google Adwords, Google Adsense, Google Analytics , YouTube partners

Using Google Adwords to Drive Targeted Traffic: Traffic is the biggest well-known secret to generate wealth in the internet based business or E-commerce. That is what every website wants and needs. The main goal of every website is to be visited and to be viewed. To make your website beautiful and attractive, professional and outstanding designs, money and countless hours of developing them is needed. Without traffic, everything is useless. Every visit (traffic) denotes a potential customer, which means sales, which in return signifies profit. Many websites have made good money by concentrating on a certain niche or sub-niches while other websites have collapsed as a result of no traffic.

Using Money to Make Money: "If you want money, you have to spend money" is a common notion of many people, particularly business owners. This is the main idea of business and you can spend money to gain traffic by advertising. Advertising is the process of bringing customers because through it, they know that your product or company is really in existence. By using the right advertising methods, you will notice the increase of traffic to your website. With a high volume of traffic or even with a small percentage of that traffic, it could turn into buying customers. Currently, the best advertising program that is worth every cent is Google Adwords. As a proof of its popularity, many online businesses use the service.

With Adwords, you will be paying a certain amount depending on the number of keywords your ad is sensitive to. Every time a person searches in Google, the keyword or keywords which are used generate the advertisement on Google search. This method ensures that the right traffic you want will be given to your website. What is more important, your website will appear on the first page of search engines. The money you pay to Google ensures that your target audience sees your ads. There are also other search engine networks where you can feature your website which includes sites such as Yahoo, AOL Search, AskJeeves and Netscape. Adwords campaigns that respond to searches performed by visitors are also shown on these sites. Content networks, which are non-search engine sites that feature Google Adwords, also carry your ads. However, it is subjected to the niche the site is featuring. The content network that features your ad is determined by your chosen keywords. Thus, the frequency of your ad is determined by the amount of money you are willing to spend.

Targeting Your Traffic: Laser targeting your traffic is the best way to get a good number or estimate of the traffic on conversion ratio. This is helpful especially if you know that your traffic are potential customers and all of them are interested in your online business and your products, and providing you with positive statistics. This signifies that the use of Google Adwords for your website is effectively working well.

Using keywords or keyword phrases that pertains to your online business and products for your Google Adwords campaign can drive targeted traffic to your site. You can use online tools to help you choose the right keywords which are currently in search. Through them, you could drive laser targeted traffic to your website. With Google Adwords campaign, you are certain that everyone who clicks on your ad is a potential customer. This is because you can assume that they are interested in what you have to offer them. As long as you are using the right keywords or keyword phrases in your ad, you can drive your laser targeted traffic to your site.

With the use of Google Adwords in helping boost the drive of your laser targeted traffic, the process could be at high cost, but the benefits can justify it all.

Google Analytics: Google Analytics (GA) is an online service offered by Google and is cost-free. It can generate a general statistics log for visitors to a website. Its service is more usable to marketers than Webmasters. Google Analytics is most commonly used statistics for online business owners. In 10,000 sites, almost 60% of them are using the service. It is also believed that 50% of the top one million websites on the web are also using Google Analytics. These statements prove how highly rated this service is in the online market when tracking consumer interest. Google analytics can give you the added advantage of seeing the number of people who visited your website and what they viewed. It will also help you get an idea of how to improve your website using the information you gained. Google Analytics uses first party cookies and JavaScript code in collecting data from visitors of your website to help you track your advertising campaign with relevant information. It tracks how many visitors interact with your website even if they do it anonymously, as well as where they come from, their activities on previous website and if they completed any of your set goals on the tracking system. Using Google Analytics is of immense value. One of its main advantages is that you will know the number of customers who interact with your website and how they got there. This is an excellent way to improve the flow of your site's traffic on a daily basis. Google Analytics lets you understand why and what people are visiting for. Thus, this can help you emphasize more popular products and services, thereby increasing the potential for the visitor to find the desired item and possibly buy it. Online businesses and Companies that specialize in e-commerce use Google Analytics as a very important tool because it allows them to obtain useful information that can help them improve their services and retain customers in the process. By using Google Analytics, email marketers will find out that there are better ways to tailor promotional messages. They can also understand the online interest of the audience, making shortcuts on the sales process and reducing the chances of a customer abandoning a product during the "cart phase".

For everyone who wants their online business to be successful, you have to use Google Analytics because the advantages of using this tool are enormous. It can help you improve all the aspects of your services leading to an increase in customers and overall appearance of your company website. What is more important, you can have these benefits, and increase cash flow in the process, all for free. Having it for free gives helps you understand why companies should try using Google Analytics and why you should do likewise.

Google Placement Targeting: One of the favorite ways online business owners use Google Pay Per Click is by Google Placement Targeting. It allows you to choose the websites featured in Google AdSense Program where you can place the ads that you selected.

Google Adsense: Google AdSense Program accepts thousand of websites every day. So, it's time for you to know Google Placement Tool and Content Bully and know how to use it.

Before you start using Google AdSense services, you need to know first the Google policies and the terms of use. You have to read all the details that are written on the site and then click the boxes if you agree with the information stated on them. Every individual is allowed to have a single approval AdSense account. Another thing to remember is you must not abuse the system by clicking your own ads. Finally, click the appropriate checkbox if you agree.

YouTube Partners: Most of the YouTube users have no idea what YouTube partner program is. A YouTube partner program is a type of online partnership where an individual teams up with YouTube to gain some benefits. It is a process of people making money using the YouTube website. As a partner, an individual is allowed to post banners and ads on the side of his video and earn money from them. YouTube partners are also allowed to upload videos longer than 10 minutes. To become a YouTube partner, you must have an account and have at least a video enabled for advertising. You also have to visit YouTube Getting Started Guide for more information and enable your videos for monetization. It is also important to mention that many people earn much money today from you YouTube as a result of becoming a partner. Moreover, an individual can also promote your business online by creating his own business channel on YouTube. This will also allow you to build larger audience, be able to rank in Google, reach many customers and earn much money.

Benefits of YouTube Partnership: YouTube offers a myriad of benefits to a number of people as well as to businesses. Besides delivering videos in higher resolution, there are still many things to be expected especially from YouTube Partnership.

First, YouTube will give you opportunity to earn revenue. A small profit is earned every time someone clicks on the videos especially where there is an embedded Google Adsense advertisement. With this in mind, you just have to comply with the requirements such as no copyright issues and following the YouTube's guidelines and Terms of Use. Second, advance access to the Insight tool is provided. It is through this medium, you will be able to optimize and maximize the reach of your videos. The benefit that comes in the third place is protection of your content. There are no risks for your content to be corrupted. With this advantage, you can brand your channel effectively since exclusive options are provided.

Insight: This tool is beneficial in a way that it provides you with pertinent information that is crucial to your online business. Its coverage usually includes the daily, monthly and annual video statistics. Besides this, it also tells you who and where your viewers are, how people get to know your video and many more.

Annotations: Videos posted in YouTube can be more interesting and fun when there are commentary interactions among viewers. This is possible with annotations wherein text bubbles are inserted or incorporated with your video after the upload. These can make your channel more engaging while linking to other YouTube videos. With annotations, there is the risk that you can lead your viewers away from the video itself. To prevent such occurrence, gain control on the bubble type and color. Moreover, also manage the time and where these annotations can pop up.

Other key features of YouTube include: It allows you to add captions and subtitles to your video. YouTube can also help you figure out the most sought keywords. It is also very easy to search for people's commentaries with comment search.

SEO & Link Building

As you optimize your website to obtain a higher ranking in search engines, you must not only be doing the "big things" that can influence the ranking. Remember, there are "little things" that you must not leave behind as they can be a great determining factor. Some worthy piece that you should keep in mind are as follows:

Bold Keywords: This may sound a bit off and old-fashioned but having words in bold print won't harm you and your ranking. Besides, the keywords you emphasize and put in bold can catch the attention of your readers and will likely use such words as anchor text when they visit or link to your site. Remember, you don't need to make all keywords bold throughout your site. Doing it once or twice in a page is fine.

Deep Linking: Search engines are getting smarter and they simply can identify if your site is worthy or not. If your backlinks point to different pages of your website, search engines will recognize that your site has significance in almost all areas. However, if it is only your landing page that is being linked into, search engines will tagged it site as a "weak." website. With this, you need to make sure that your backlinks are directed to different pages on your website. Social bookmarking: To help you create and develop useful links, make sure that your page can easily be bookmarked by your readers. To do this, there are several widgets that you can use and add into your website. This will allow you to make a big difference and achieve real success with your SEO in the process. Remember, link building is about having sites pointing back or linking to your website. You will gain more authority if you have more links but never forget that links were not created equal. To explain this deeper, let me use the following categories to explain it:

- Regular Value Links
- Mid Value Links
- Authority Links

You certainly know that all website owners and bloggers want Authority links since they are more relevant and beneficial. Keep in mind that mid-value links are commonly found in the middle. Moreover, authority links have several mid value links and more often than not, they contain links that point to inbound links. With that being said, it determines the page rank.

Furthermore, on page SEO determines the ranking factors from

♦ Headline tags

♦ Bold/Underlined/italicized keyword phrases

♦ Anchor Text Links and Off Page SEO

♦ Quantity of inbound links and Authority of those links.

There are two types of Inbound Links:

Regular   Inbound   Link   e.g. http://www.thesecretcodetosuccessandwealth.com

Anchor Text Inbound Link e.g. Online Business Book

The anchor text will inform search engines what a certain page is all about. Such links are the best but trying to branch out is also good. Keep in mind that page rank 0-3 is the regular value, page rank 4-5 is the mid value while page rank 6 and above is the authority link. With this being said, it is important to build links that will directly point to your main website. This will certainly increase your site's authority. More so, you need to build inbound links to improve the authority of your website's inbound links. For instance, you must not forget to send inbound links to Web 2.0 sites and article directories since these two possess great authorities. This will be improving your website's position in authority and search engines. It is also important that you build lists of news media, bloggers and journalists as you will at some point have to contact them and build a business relationship with them. In addition, to avoid your links being affected by Google updates, make sure that you only offer quality and unique contents and they should not be spam.

Here are the 12 checklist you need to consider when exploring link building:

- Is it a relevant website?
- Does it have well written content?
- Can you easily contact the owner?
- Does the website have real people?
- Does the website have good inbound links?
- Is it a well established website?
- Is the website linking out to many websites?
- Do they regularly update the website?
- Is the website score very good on Alexa, Google Page rank and Compete?
- Does the website interview others for opinions or studies?
- Does the website publish reviews or resources?
- Does the website perform better on keyword searches?

Article Marketing, Article Spinning and Business Blogging

Benefits of Article Writing & Marketing: All of us have probably heard about writing articles since it is the best way to create a website. However, we may not know the right approach of taking this or we may not realize the benefits of writing articles. In result, chances of taking this step all by yourself may create problems such as not generating any revenue in the long run.

There are two facts when it comes to the benefits of writing articles which are part of your marketing tools. The first one is that through writing articles, you can create and build backlinks that will help you in search engine ranking. The second fact is that you can directly send traffic to your website by merely writing quality contents. These two things should be understood however, one must realize that having a good content is the main key for effective articles. It also means having valuable information that will trigger readers to click on the links and visit your website eventually. In addition, your articles should be submitted properly to article directories, blogs etc to create successful backlinks.

However, after writing quality content with proper links that will bring your readers into your website, you can then submit all articles on top article sites using article upload tool. By using this tool, the possibility of writing two additional variations of sentences is high. From there, <u>Article Spinner</u> will take care of the rest. The software will create different variations of the quality content thus giving you several articles from just one unique article. With this, expect more visitors to your website.

Insights for Article Content: After you have finished writing articles and being able to submit them using the right tool, you will eventually see results in spite of having a good or bad content. However, the better your contents are, the greater the outcome will be. With this, you need to realize and learn some key points about article writing before you go through it.

Furthermore, you must know that articles are not just for backlinks. More so, you must not think that contents with enough and flowery words, along with embedded links, are already good. Think about this! How will your readers react to a boring and useless content? Instead of making such mistake, focus on what people would like to read. Give them quality and informative articles. This will not only generate traffic to your site but will also build your credibility as a writer. Another key to being successful in this stuff is that each article must be introductory. Remember, your readers may not know you or the niche of your site. With this, you need to come up with an informative and easy-to-understand write-up. This will help you build connection with your target market. Lastly, make sure that your articles are valuable and yet open-ended. This will entice readers to visit your site again, know everything about you and find answers to the topic in question. As a result, many people will end up clicking your links repeatedly. With this, you can expect more traffic and certainly, more profit.

Article Spinning: Article upload tool is definitely one of the most appreciated tools that would help you both in creating backlinks for your search engine ranking and for having more traffic on your site. However, before you continue on using such tool, you should know and understand the essentials of article spinning.

The idea of using article spinning is that it helps you write many variations of sentences from one article. With this, you will come up with a number of unique articles having the same thought. Why is this beneficial? You surely know that search engines such us Google, Yahoo and Bing will penalize you for duplicated contents. To avoid such scenario, article spinning is at your disposal to help you obtain similar unique articles for various platforms. Isn't this great? However, the flow of sentences is the hardest thing that most people would come across in using article spinning. As a result, you will need to write second and third variations of sentences for you to have the same thought like the first variations. By doing so, you will likely end up with a content that has a great flow of sentences.

Moreover, for you to have the best spin articles, try not changing the beginning and end of each sentence. With this, you can have an assurance that your sentences will flow naturally leading to an article with an excellent flow of story. As you become more inclined with article spinning, you will get more comfortable with it and that will help you hit the right notes. One thing that you should also know about article spinning is that it won't take much time spinning sentences especially those that are a bit long. Spinning sentences that are shorter are hard to spin. So make sure that as you write your sentences, make them long enough to express all your thoughts but not much longer where readers will have a hard time following it. One last thing that you should keep in mind is that the more you practice article spinning, the easier things will become. From there, expect to be successful as a result of it. So, get started with your article spinning now and earn your profit in no time!

Business Blogging: Everything you post on the website intended for search engine marketing is expected to come from the Chief Executive Officer (CEO). This is also the same if you are managing small business and telling people that what they are reading is from the CEO. That will perhaps sound pretentious and pompous for you. However, when you give your customers direct messages from the CEO, it will definitely be a great boost to your business especially if you operate an industry with multiple locations or you own a company with 25 or more employees. At present, the idea of sending direct messages from the CEO to customers is one thing to realize because it is not exactly groundbreaking. In spite of everything, big businesses are doing this along with other forms of direct communication and stockholder reports. Then again, your website is where you should vary from this approach. This is where your customers should feel that they are communicating with the "Big Boss" in a direct manner so you have to give them a chance.

If you are the CEO, you can do this by posting contributions on your company's blog every so often! This will really do a lot to give your blog more momentum, especially if you have someone else from your company who is running the blog and have done a good job making it popular.

Logging onto the blog often and responding to the comments that readers have left are another ways that would make your readers feel as though they are interacting with you. The majority of successful blogs nowadays get the most out of the interaction with readers in the comments section. The impact would even be felt more if this interaction comes from the CEO.

Lastly, your customers will have an opportunity to interact with you by opening an online "Q & A" session with the

CEO every now and then. This will also help a lot by increasing the probability of your customers being loyal to you. As a result, you will find their loyalty beneficial to your online business.

Viral Blogging: The power of community blogging is influenced by a viral blog platform. When you say community blogging, there is an assembly of writers who are posting content on the similar blogging platform while the same domain name is being used. Helping affiliate marketers, Internet marketers, online business owners, bloggers, and other e-commerce businesses sufficiently are the main purpose of <u>viral blogging</u>. Apart from that, it is also possible to quickly advertise their products or services online. The power of viral blog cannot be under estimated as it helps viral bloggers to expand and reach a global audience to promote their products or service locally.

Although there are some blogging platforms that have a viral blogging model, they still differ in usability and structure. Many users find several platforms that are difficult to set-up because they require in depth technical abilities. However, other systems require little to no setup and are ready for use. If you are new to the online business arena and blogging, using a viral blog may be a good option. Nearly all technical setups are removed depending on your choice of blogging platform, which allows you to simply sign-up and start blogging. Leveraging the power of domain recognition and authority are the other benefits of viral blogging system. Receiving traffic to a certain website usually takes a while to start when an individual comes online and starts a new blog. This happens for the reason that their new domain name has no authority or seniority in the search engines.

As a new blogger, you'll begin to receive your first streams of search engine traffic if you have consistently posted to your blog for at least ninety days. To gain website authority, you have to do an extensive amount of backlinking. By doing this while posting consistently to your blog for six months to a year, you'll begin to get significant blog traffic. As a beginner, this work is quite extreme and that can at times end up making him or her to give up. If you have the money, you can always pay others to blog for you. A viral blogging platform is already recognized by the search engines. It has also the authority of a seasoned domain name. Because of the domain age and its many users, the authority of it comes from a large number of backlinks. The specific keyword will rapidly get ranked and indexed in the search engines whenever a person blogs on this platform.

This is done within twenty-four hours in some cases. Normally, it takes three weeks to a month for a content to rank in the first page of search engines. The power of a viral blogging system is huge and it is the easiest and quickest way for a content to get ranked on the first page of search engines. The more users that blog on the platform, the more ranking power and authority your domain will obtain. As a result, you will receive more traffic. Thousands of bloggers on one domain are more powerful than one blogger in the same domain.

Affiliate Marketing & Tracking: There are large numbers of individuals who own and operate their online businesses all over the world. Both large and small businesses have one goal, and it is to make money. Unfortunately, several businesses find it hard to do that on their own. However, you may be able to benefit from the creation of an affiliate program if you own a business and you are struggling to make profit. You can do this by examining <u>affiliate tracking software</u> which is an important affiliate program to use for tracking the sales of your affiliate partners. Many business owners incorrectly believe that they cannot profit from the creation of an affiliate program although there is a large number of businesses that are able to do this. Most of these business owners believe this information even though it is untrue and has no precise source. This may also cost you money if you can't afford to lose. However, by understanding how your online business can use and take advantage of the affiliate tracking software and affiliate program, you will surely be on your way to generating more income as it is one of the best things to do.

How to Get Started: People engage in advertising other people's products which is also known as affiliate marketing. To bring visitors to buy those products or services; we "implement" Internet marketing strategies. Advertising online is one of the most efficient ways to advertise and affiliate marketing is just a different way of advertising.

The Internet marketing strategies of big companies and affiliate marketing are both great ways to use and increase product sales.

Affiliate Networks: You always want to ensure that you are able to sign up with different affiliate networks whether you are incorporated as a (LTD, LLC, Inc., etc.) or just a self-employed individual. This is important if you have that desire to find products and services to promote. <u>CPA networks</u> should be the first kind of <u>affiliate network</u> that you have to sign up with. <u>Clickbank</u> is also an available "cost per sale" network. With it, you can only get paid when a person makes a purchase. <u>LinkShare</u> and <u>Commission</u>

Junction are both networks that have a mix of both types of offers.

Affiliate Programs: Collaboration between a business owner and a website owner, web publisher, or publisher is defined as affiliate programs. The goal of this partnership is to help a business generate more sales and it benefits both parties. Links and banners which are used on your affiliate website are the advertisement campaigns for your affiliate program. You are going to give a commission to the affiliate as banners and links lead to a sale. On the other hand, you need an affiliate tracking software to know whether a sale is just something that was generated through one of your affiliates or a traditional sale. A software program that will work with your own affiliate program is what affiliate tracking software is all about. Once you have signed up with many software programs, it will require you to create links and banners that differ with each other. By means of unique affiliate ID codes, these banners will often be tagged. Your affiliates can be distinguished through these codes. They also allow affiliate to properly be rewarded. As a result, it will bring traffic to your online business.

Obviously, using affiliate tracking software does not really need special requirements. On the other hand, having your own affiliate program is advisable. Anyone can benefit from affiliate program just as with affiliate tracking software. By using these two, both large and small online business owners will benefit from them. Due to the sales increase they will bring, small business owners could possibly benefit the most. Generally, it is almost guaranteed that small businesses will profit from even a slight increase in sales. An online business owner can benefit from the use of an affiliate program just like how the majority of them profit from it.

You may also be able to make money as an affiliate, if, by any means, you do not sell any services or products. With this, you'll end up getting commission for helping other business increase sales. You and your business could make a considerable profit whichever way you choose. Examining what those businesses do is also essential. You will find that it is a good idea to participate in businesses that specialize in selling services or products. This is because of record sales that an affiliate website generates, and affiliate program relies on an affiliate tracking software.

List Building

In list building, the reality is that the quality of your list will determine how much you will earn. Therefore, the common notion that having many on your list will give you a greater chance of having bigger profit is not true. However, if you really want to have bigger profits, then focus on the quality of your list and not on the quantity. These are some of the helpful ways of building excellent list:

Sorting Quality Customers from Your Website: If you have attracted many visitors on your website, you may get hold of them and get their contact details. They could be potential customers because they seem interested with your services since they browsed your website.

Work on Pop-Ups: Pop-ups may be annoying to visitors but having pop-ups in a website is a reliable tool in building an excellent list.

Have Squeeze Pages: Squeeze pages are popular in websites because it requires the name and email address of the visitors before they could access the website. This is a sure way of obtaining a superior list of potential clients as this method converts very well.

Place Opt-In Boxes: Opt-in boxes are areas on web pages where the visitors could enter their contact information. Placing opt-in box on your page is a good way to encourage your visitors to provide their details which is a good source for your list building.

Apart from using the provided methods in building excellent list, you must have captivating web content. This is because no one would visit your site if your content is not attractive enough for the readers and thus you will not be able to get their information.

The frequency of having your website visited may increase your conversion rate up to 20% or more. This depends on how the visitors landed on your website; it could be through links, Ad Words, Google search result etc... Conversion rate optimizes your web page and makes your profit or visibility to clients higher.

Tips on How to Consistently Obtain High Quality Conversions

Please Your Potential Clients: Try to offer your prospective clients some free trials or materials. Let them experience the beauty or benefit of what you are offering. This is one of the most effective ways of marketing, having the clients experience your services first hand. Through this, you will be able to build excellent listing rather than asking for their names and contact details from the onset.

This method is better than self-praising style such as press releases, headlines and other similar things. When your potential clients like what they have seen and experienced in your trial product, they will eventually sign up to the guest list. The possibility of having them as a client is huge.

Mind Your Branding: Having an excellent list does not mean that all of your prospective clients are captivated by your website. Thus, you must have a certain branding, a trusted name when it comes to being an excellent supplier. Try to touch base with your prospective clients at least once a week by offering them some freebies initially. You may offer them some products for sale on your fourth email. Just remember not to offer any sales on the earlier stage as you want to build the relationship first. As an online business owner, you must establish an image of being mindful to your clients before offering them something.

Acquiring excellent list for business is not an easy task. Therefore, one must know how to take care of the prospective list of clients and protect his business' image once you are able to secure quality list. This will greatly help your business and improve your lifestyle.

Online Auctions

The strength of online auction is that it is not restricted by time. Buyers could place their bids anytime since internet can be accessed anytime of the day and this makes the business model more efficient. It could cater to huge number of sellers and buyers.

In online auction, the lists of products that are available for bidding are on for some days which are visible to the bidder. This provides the bidders ample time to search, decide and bid for the products that they want. The convenience of this set up attracts huge number of bidders.

Strength of online auction is that, it is not limited based on location. Both the sellers and the buyers can participate as long as they have access to internet anywhere. This accessibility makes the online auction more valued as a choice to both participants and prospective participants.

Online auction websites save much time and money for both the sellers and buyers. The costs in movement are minimized or eliminated in online auction. There's no need for the participants to travel to or to ship the products to the auction venue. Everything just happens very quickly. You can buy products for sale online through online auction website including domain auctions.

For the record, online auction has the biggest number of bidders and again this all boils down to convenience. The accessibility of internet makes the bidding easier and attractive to participants because the seller could post several products and reach huge number of bidders all over the globe. As for the bidders, it is the convenience of choosing from wide range of products that they cannot find in the usual auction set up.

Also, in online auction the sellers provide some guarantee with their products and with the money of the buyer. This security is not normally provided in an ordinary auction, once the bidder has given their bids, they are no longer refundable. This is the main reason why many buyers avoid the conventional set up. Indeed, the convenience, affordability and security that online auction provides continue to draw large number of participants. This business model is poised to dominate the auction industry.

CPA Networks

In promoting CPA (Cost Per Action) offers, you will get paid for the lead generation or for the actual sales. This could be through emails sent, credit reports and other similar things. Either way, the use of banner advertising, pay per click, Facebook marketing, Twitter marketing to drive huge traffic to a product or service you are promoting is a good method. In essence, you can use the strategies provided in Banner Ad Blueprint to drive high traffic to any of the offers hosted by CPA Networks.

There are many ways to make money through CPA unlike in traditional affiliate marketing in which you must have "sales" to earn money. The latter could be tedious at times.

These are the various ways on how to make money from CPA:

- Sales
- Free trials
- Leads
- Registrations
- Downloads

In a regular affiliate program, even if you direct a customer on a landing page but the customer did not buy the product, you don't earn money. It will be a disadvantage on your end if you used paid advertising to generate traffic on the website. While for CPA marketing, you earn money just by allowing your visitors to submit their email address. You may also use different methods to drive traffic on the website for free.

Generally, the actual pay out for traditional affiliate program is higher compared to CPA. Also, to illustrate the risk of affiliate marketing, if you advertised an Apple Laptop the Apple Store is giving out 1% commission. If your sale is $1,000, you will earn $10. Before going online, buyers usually go around to shop. So that is the normal risk with CPA. Even if this is the case, making money with CPA is indeed easier. This is because, as has been previously indicated in traditional affiliate programs no actual sale means no earnings. With CPA, it is generally easier to persuade the visitors to sign up or provide their email since they don't have to pay anything and instantly you already have earnings. The payout might be lower but constant earnings will give you higher amount of income.

The key with CPA is persuading your visitors to become a part of what you are offering by providing their basic details such as their email address. This is the huge advantage of CPA; in the current economic climate giving out email is easier than giving away money.

Getting Accepted into CPA Networks: CPA Networks require different information from their affiliate applicants. They even differ in referring applicants. Some call them "affiliates" while others refer to them as "publishers". The term "advertiser" is solely used for companies who are running the offers.

These are the information that you must have before applying to any CPA Network:

Name to Use: This is the first thing that they will ask when you apply as an affiliate. You can use either your personal name or your business name. It is highly recommended to use a business name because you are sending the message that you are serious in doing business.

Payee's Name: You may use your name or your company name.

Method of Payment: CPA networks usually pay through wire transfer or check. Wire transfer of payment is normally exclusive for high volume affiliates while check payment is usually for regular or beginner affiliates. Choose check payment if you are just starting up.

Provide Contact Number and Address: Provide a contact number that has a professional voicemail message. This will create a professional impression to the CPA Network that you applied to should you not be available to answer their calls.

As for the address you may use either your personal or business address.

Give Easy to Recall Instant Messenger Handle: There are some networks that are requiring IM handle. Give the one which is easy to recall, an email username is the easiest to remember.

Taxation Details: If you applied as an individual, your Tax Number will also serve as your Social Security Number. If you applied as a company then use your Employer Identification Number or EIN or as to whatever is applicable in your country.

Strategically List Your Experience Level: If you are new to CPA Marketing, don't just put zero experience. Instead, indicate 0 to 6 months experience or 6 months to 1 year experience whichever is applicable.

The strategic way of listing your experience will not harm you in anyway. The reason for doing this is if you listed that you are totally inexperienced it means that you do not have the capacity to make money in CPA and therefore you may not be accepted unto the network.

Expenditure in Advertising and Earning Status: Most of the CPA Networks require you to indicate your spending on ads per day as well as your earning status.

Again, you have to be strategic as they are looking for a range of at least $300 day to $5,000 per month. As for the earnings, they need a figure of at least $5,000 per month. These minimum figures are decent enough to make you get in the door.

Ways to promote offers: For the method on how you intend to promote the network offers, list SEO (Search Engine Optimization) or PPC (Pay per Click), social media, blogging etc.

In case you already have an email list, select e-mail list. The CPA Network may ask you if you have a website. So you need to include one or more. If they ask you for the name of your website, do not fill it out yet until you are able to create at least your basic website. If you have not yet created the website, try to sort it out soon.

Also, be prepared as to where your traffics are coming from. This could be from US, UK, Asia etc...

Other Networks You are Connected With: The more networks you have worked in the past, the better. You may include that you have worked for Clickbank, Commission Junction etc. Once you have submitted the completed form, wait for them to review and get back to you as they will suggest. Call the attention of the CPA Network in case that you haven't been contacted. Follow them up and inform them to expedite the process in order for you to get started. The CPA Network usually likes this initiative if showed by the applicants. When a representative contacts you, he or she will verify the details that you have provided in your form. Make sure that your answers will be consistent with what you have provided on the form. Answer in details. You will receive a response immediately if you are accepted, either by phone or by email. In case that you get accepted and the Network is US based and you are also from US, you have to submit your W-9 tax information through fax or email. If you get accepted by a Canadian Networks then no need to submit it.

Make sure that you submit your relevant tax details for the Country where you are; otherwise you won't get paid even if you have huge earnings.

Benefits of using various Advertising Options including Media Buying, PPV, PPC, CPC, CPL Traffic, Banner Advertising, CPM, CPA etc.

The use of advertising network is mutually beneficial for the advertisers and the publishers. It paves way to link the advertisers and publishers who are interested in advertisement hosting. Through this the advertisers could easily tap huge number of target audience to increase their traffic and sales while the publishers earn income through hosting the ads.

Easy Management of Pay for Results Campaign: The advertising network makes the management of pay for result campaign for all types of internet marketing as it makes the flow easy for the advertisers. Also, it allows the advertisers to reach bigger target audience by effective online advertising such as email campaigns, display advertising, search engine marketing and social media advertising campaigns.

The publisher could generate additional income through hosting ads and use of the advertising network to manage campaigns and provide tools to help the publishers identify the highest paying campaigns. This provides the ability to maximize profit, since the advertiser only pays for results.

This set up helps the publishers a lot because they could easily move in hosting ads and use the advertising network in managing and identifying the highest paying campaigns. The publishers are able to maximize their profit.

Solid Marketing Plans: To achieve the best results, there must be a solid marketing blue print. Online business owners (entrepreneurs) should maximize the use of online tools that could reach their target audience to generate traffic to their website. More often than not, business owners do not have either the knowledge or the time to create an excellent campaign for their site. In this case, hiring a professional to handle the task is the best option

Email Marketing: Email marketing works best in direct marketing industry because target clients prefer email messages from companies regarding their offers or sales. This strategy gives direct connection to the clients and encourages them to establish loyal relationship.

Cost Per Click: The Media Trust's CPC bidding platform has a reliable tool for linking advertisers to new customers. The edge of this platform is that the text ads both for the CPC bidding and the winning bidder are generated based on real time. Advertisers pay only for qualified customers that are delivered to their landing pages. The text ads are created by Media Trust's marketing specialists to help the advertisers in generating leads more effectively and in achieving better sales. The text ads could include creative graphics that are displayed to your target audience that have high probability of responding to the ads. Media channels in use include emails, media buys, banner, contextual, search, incentives and social media.

Performance Exchange: This is an advertising network under Media Trust that is very easy to use. Performance Exchange has all the tools that you need for setting budget, placing of bids and providing the result of all your marketing efforts.

If you are really serious about improving your marketing result, Media Trust ads is highly recommended. It makes regulatory compliance for email marketing easy plus it is monitored for CANSPAM compliance. It could really boost your online sales. For in depth information about the benefits of CANSPAM, you may browse their website.

Media Buying: Online advertising is one of the effective means of gaining an upper hand in online business. However, if you are not diligent enough, you may end up having huge cost in advertising with only small amount of return in investment. This scenario could be avoided by working on with inexpensive online ads that could bring you huge profits.

These are the three ways on how to work on "inexpensive" online ads. These will surely help you to achieve the profit that you want.

Capitalize on your time and skills in using free ads: With online advertising, you have to think out of the box and be discerning what kind of advertising will produce the best result. Traditional paid advertising are known to be useful however, you can be creative and try free advertising. With free advertising, you can make use of customer interaction and SEO to generate high traffic on your website.

Your only investment with free advertising is your time and your skills.

Using Your Money to Generate More Income: One of the best ways to bring new traffic and new customers your way is with promotions and deals. Although you will make less money on a per-product basis when you run specials and give customers big deals, this will pay off in the long run, as you will be able to bring many people to your website who might not otherwise have visited. Investing in promotions and deals is a sure way to attract more customers. Definitely, people get attracted to good promotions and deals.

Initially, this could be costly because you have to cash out, but in the long run you will reap the benefits and that is more income for you. Money begets money thus it is important to know when and where you will spend your money to generate higher income.

Know the Power of Pay Per Click (PPC) Advertising: PPC ad campaign helps you to know the amount of money that you will need each month. It helps you to determine the costs that you will accrue based on clicked ads. Considering this, you will be able to estimate and adjust your budget based on the results that you get.

In every business there is a risk and that's the same with online advertising. Hence, you have to assess whether a certain online advertisement could make or lose you money. It's your decision.

Don't go for an online advertisement that you think could make your money go down the drain. Instead, be creative and use other options that will not cost you so much money. Be smarter and try to exhaust other means such as network, time and skills. This way, you will be able to achieve results for only minimal costs.

Pay Per View (PPV): The efficiency of PPV (Pay per View) is not known to many marketers. It is not widely used because only few understand its power to generate significant results in online marketing. Contrary to common belief, PPV is not your ordinary PPC; it can even outperform PPC advertising in so many ways.

The primary advantage of PPV is its solid network of potential customers. Even though there is a difference between PPV network to PPC network, but the huge ones usually generate as many as 20 million users. These 20 million users are active sources since they agree to view the advertisements.

When any keyword or website that you bid on is triggered by one of these 20 million people, your advertisement is going to be displayed for them to see. It will be displayed directly, not just as an advertisement, but as a website, landing page, and so on. In itself, this means that you're going to have a lot more control over your advertising and the effect it can potentially have. If the website or keyword that has been bid on was done by one of the 20 million viewers, your website will be advertised for all of them to see. This will be a direct showing of your website in a form of landing page, actual website, etc… This means that you have a better control of your advertisement and its effect to viewers.

Even though <u>PPV advertising</u> has the capacity to touch base with huge number of users, it is able to maintain its affordability. If this would change in the future, there would be more people to start bidding for the same keywords or sites, but currently it continues to provide 1st rank bids for as low as $ 0.01 for various very popular sites and keywords.

This rate is still affordable given that there were changes in rates in PPV advertising networks.

Furthermore, PPV is more liberal with using the PPV advertising compared to many rules being imposed by PPC operators.

Relatively speaking, PPV is still new and its future advantages are yet to be seen. Currently, it provides immense advantages for the marketers to use and that is generating huge traffic to their sites at affordable rates.

With this, it is expected that the number of PPV users will increase given this opportunity and currently, that is what's happening. As long as you are willing to learn the ropes of PPV and invest a little in their advertising, you will soon reap more than what you have invested. As you familiarize yourself more with its ropes, your earnings will surely increase and you will be able to see the immense potential of PPV advertising.

Direct CPV: <u>Direct Cost per view</u> is a new Cost Per View advertising network, that has tons of high quality traffic which can be delivered to your website. One of the best things about this network is that you can go as low as .004c per view. DirectCPV.com has a great video on their website. I recommend that you view it also. You can also check out

<u>Media Traffic</u> which is a great CPV Contextual advertising network. You can also use tracking software like <u>Tracking202</u> and <u>Prosper202</u> to keep track of what's going on in your CPV advertising. The most recommended Cost Per View network is <u>Traffic Vance</u>. They have high standards in their application requirements. To secure an account with them, you have to submit an ID picture, a credit card authorization form and a $1000 deposit to your Traffic Vance account. They generate traffic through their website GameVance.com.

Pay Per Click (PPC) / CPC: If you have studied and understand SEO, to a point where you feel comfortable that you could use your knowledge and the <u>Webfire</u> tools at your disposal to carry out SEO on any website of yours in order to get to the top of search engine ranking, your next step will be figuring out how you can turn this knowledge into some sort of income.

If your main focus is to promote your business through SEO, that would be easy. However, if you will be more creative and want to earn income through SEO, you have to acquaint yourself with the various tools that could help you to accomplish this.

There are many ways to make money online but the easiest and the most popular tool is using PPC (Pay Per Click) to your website. PPC ads are the ads that are placed on a website. The creator of the ads earns money if the ad has been viewed by an online visitor. The best known PPC is Google Adwords and Google Adsense; however, there are many other PPCS ads that you can use on your site.

PPC Platforms: A highly recommended PPC network which will increase your ROI is <u>Clicksor.</u> Clicksor matches the viewers to your website based on the products that you are offering. Clicksor helps you build different targeting options to achieve this. You can check out Clicksor's website by visiting www.ClickSor.com.

Another network that has established excellent reputation in generating huge traffic and at the same time providing a cutting –edge advertising solutions is AdOn Network. This network has a unique set up process; you may check their website at www.AdOnNetwork.com to see the complete details.

AdBlade is one of the biggest advertising platforms that are catering for premium local and national branded websites. The only thing with AdBlade is that you cannot perform targeting however using this network is proven to be profitable. If you are interested with AdBlade visit their link at www.AdBlade.com. You may also watch their video and join the game.

PPC ads provide you with the edge on packaging the content of your website to the level you desire. You will make money through the targeted traffic that you deliver to the website as viewers are required to click the provided links. With online marketing, you can create many web pages and make money from various sources all at once. That's why some online business owners make millions of dollars because they sign up to all these networks and as they are generating good return, they are spending more to earn more. If you are in position to do the same, do not be surprised if your revenue increases astronomically.

PPC is not meant for everyone. If you are really interested in building your website and exploring the various contents that you want or if you are keen to monetize your site then PPC is worth trying.

Currently, establishing an E-Commerce website is not what it used to be. Competitors are just around the corner and are driven to gaining the upper hand. So the trick is to apply all the methods that you know to secure targeted leads and increase your online business sales.

Most of the people who venture into e-commerce and online marketing are in it to generate income. This requires time, energy and resources and no one will go into it just to have some fun. There are some who take online business easily but there are more who take it very seriously. You will see that many websites are using various options to ensure that they will profit at any given day. Like in any other businesses, if you do not have traffic, you don't have business. Traffic shows the number of people that have interests in what you are offering. The larger the number of visitors to your website, the greater the chance you have of making sales. Remember that customers are the ones that provide you money. Find them and keep them.

When you get into online business, you need to focus on generating traffic because this will be the lifeblood of your business. This will also help you to regain all the investments that you made to stay in business.

Making Money Out of Your Traffic: The most effective way to earn money through your traffic is advertising. The internet generates much traffic every day. These could be people that are just looking for some information or they could be searching for solution to their needs. This is where advertising comes in, as many people browsing the internet are searching for one or the other. The internet has been proven to be a highly reliable tool in finding all sorts of products. It makes the world very interconnected. For example, you can advertise your product in London but have a buyer from Australia. Traffic generation could be a hard task as you have to compete with huge number of sites out there. If you know the effective methods on how to do it and become successful in it, you will see unlimited possibilities, which includes generating revenue from your constant flow of traffic.

So briefly, the more traffic you can get to your website, the more desirable you become. This means that more people will view your website because you have already created the impression that your site is profitable and thus established. This could be all done through strategic advertising. You need to use this to your advantage. If you have good traffic, you will also have good number of prospective clients that are willing to pay. Also, there are traffics that can be redirected to other sponsored links and that could earn you more money. This strategy is known as "pay-per-click". As the name implies, you will earn based on how many clicks the visitors make on the advertised link.

Affiliate Programs: Affiliate program is another tested method in generating income. With this, you can link with other more established online companies and sites; you will earn income by having part of the sales made by the traffic from your site. The basic thing with Affiliate program is that it redirects visitors to other sites that you linked up with if you do not have what they are looking for. This kind of transactions can be tracked by many programs due to the site linking. The benefit of Affiliate program is that you don't have to be the owner of the products to generate income. You just have to market the link of the affiliate website which has the products that customers are looking for and you get certain percentage from sale that has been made. This is indeed a good way to earn money from your traffic. There are many ways to generate earnings from your traffic. You will find many tips, information and support systems in the internet to make your website profitable. All you need is hard work, the burning desire to succeed and knowledge of ways to make money online which has been covered in this book.

Use of Social Media (Twitter, Facebook, YouTube, Pinterest, Slide share, LinkedIn, My Space)

The use of Social Networking websites for your online business is part of your search engine optimization and marketing. Most likely you are a member of social networking websites like Facebook, Twitter, etc given that they are very popular. However, there is a big difference between being just a member and being an active participant in online discussions and other networking groups. You have to make the most out of your social networking experience by establishing your presence and contacts. The first thing to do to make the social networking work for you is to acquaint yourself with the social networking community that you are in. You have to know the ins and outs of the community by studying the features of the websites, checking out the terms and conditions of use as you would not want to be banned from using the network. This provides the dos and don'ts in the networking site.

There are some that have few rules such as MySpace but there are also some that have established rules like Facebook, Twitter. Some of the networking websites policies provide certain restrictions in terms of uploading of pictures, videos, contents etc for the protection of the users. It is important to know the rules of the networking websites that you are in so that you will be guided accordingly. One of the beauty of reviewing the policies and contents of the social site where you join is that you become aware of the benefits that you can gain from being a member. Since there are also opportunities linked to marketing and advertising using the social media, it is very important that you explore those opportunities and use them effectively. Such opportunities extend beyond creating your online business page and marketing to customers as this is where your potential customers are. It is very important that you carry out a search to find the relevant networks which you can join to tap into the marketing opportunities. There are so many income-generating business opportunities linked to Facebook, Twitter, and YouTube etc and that I will specifically take on with those that I will be coaching as they are very diverse, lucrative and enriching topics and therefore cannot be covered specifically in this book. However, feel free to contact me to know how I might help you in learning those specific strategies.

With this, you already have some ideas on how to make use of the networking sites to your advantage. It is up to you on how you will do this. Whether you want to do due diligence and research what each networking sites has to offer or just jump to the opportunities, it would be your choice.

Social Bookmarking and Creating Product Review website

Social Bookmarking is a collection of websites created by various internet users which is used to increase traffic to a website. This has been proven to be very helpful in making a website noticeable to online users. Thus, there are many bookmarking services available online.

Social Bookmarking has been a popular tool to SEO professionals because it is a reliable tool in increasing traffic flow to a website. Increase in traffic flow drives more internet viewers because of the popularity factor. So if you want to attract attention to your website and establish your online presence, social bookmarking could really help you.

When an internet viewer signs up to a website and likes it, they usually do bookmarking instead of tagging it. Bookmarking is done when the user wants to include a certain site to their favorite lists or when they find your website useful. Bookmarking is somewhat similar to keywords wherein the visitors use certain word to bookmark your site. For example you search for the words reverse osmosis; the website will show you the websites that are bookmarked by site users. Thus, the many bookmarking your site got from users, the higher you will rank in search engine and this means more earnings at your end. The primary feature of Social Bookmarking is to directly and indirectly generate more traffic to your website. The main goal for the users is to bookmark your content and website. There are many companies that make simple yet effective bookmarking script to make it easier for the users and for their sited to obtain higher ranking.

In bookmarking, it is highly advisable to make accounts at well-known Bookmarking sites. You have to take note of your websites that are attracting huge visitors and bookmark them. Make sure to avoid spamming by using appropriate tags, also this will save you from being banned in different search engines.

There are many bookmarking strategies which are being used by SEO professionals for different websites. Choose the most effective bookmarking strategy for you and increase traffic to your website. If your websites become popular online, more visitors will be attracted to drop by. Also, make use of the most relevant tags only so that your website will land on the top spots of the search engines.

Currently, webmasters and bloggers are using social bookmarking submission software to build good backlinks and established traffic to their sites. This software has gained its popularity among SEO professionals because it is easy to use and generate better results. One of the well-known social bookmarking sites is the Web 2.0. Its introduction to the market paves way to creativity and makes unconventional means for the sites and the web users to interact.

In a traditional set up, a website visitor will just drop by at a website without interacting. Web 2.0 changed that paradigm as it allows everyone such as the website owners and web visitors to interact with one another. With this, it could be seen that social bookmarking software such as Web 2.0 are poised to improve the social networking arena by attracting solid traffic and generating good backlinks that could give good earnings.

The goal of social bookmarking submission software is to make it easier to arrange the bookmarks by categories and tags both for personal and public bookmarks. These social media sites could be used by anyone; they could just register and bookmark the URLs that they like. The saved bookmarks can be used for personal purposes or could be also shared with others. As to the case of public bookmarks, it is not only limited to sharing with others, it can also be viewed wherever you are so long as you have access to the internet. In the event of submitting social bookmarking sites, the search engines can visit those sites and index them. The indexed social sites with bookmarking links are being followed by search engine androids and lead the androids to these popular links. This provides the website owners opportunity to use the bookmarked websites for link building.

The submission of social bookmarking sites offers good opportunity for link building and for generating free traffic. Website owners are aware how important traffic is for a website. Even webmasters know this and they have one goal and that is to generate huge traffic to their sites because this means that there is a huge possibility for them to earn more money. Social bookmarking does not only establish link building and traffic generation, it also promotes brand awareness. Those sites that have branding are frequently visited by millions of people thus your presence on these sites will give you the opportunity to promote your brand as well. On the other hand, there are product reviews conducted online. This aims to guide or facilitate the virtual shoppers to search and decide for the right product that they will buy online. The professional reviews done for various products have huge influence in buying decision of the online visitors.

Unlike other product review, professional product reviews provide a more accurate image of the product. Providing feedback as they are and this includes the weaknesses of the products. This is the main reason why online buyers check first professional reviews before buying any products online. In retrospect, online buyers are now smarter. They make sure that they have the accurate description of the products that are not only based on the good qualities but the products' disadvantages as well. Online consumers are now more careful so that they will not be deceived.

Though professional product reviews are aimed for prospective buyers, it is also a fact that retailers also benefit from the reviews. Even though there are some negative comments, these help the retailers to review their products and position themselves strategically with their competitors. Also, product reviews generate traffic to the retailers' websites and could also be considered as a form of advertising for free.

With this, it can also be considered that professional product reviews are effective marketing tools. It provides benefits not only to prospective consumers but also to businesses who want to improve their products based on the reviews and generate more sales. However, you need to remember that it is mostly the big brands that they focus on and that should not stop you from buying from small online businesses that have very competitive prices but are yet to dominate the market.

For individuals who are looking to shop for products online, it is highly recommended that you review thoroughly the products, its features, advantages and defects before you place an order. Research thoroughly for different product reviews and make sure that you have all the information and specifications before ordering the product and deliver it at your doorsteps.

In totality, more clients and companies begin to understand the usefulness of professional reviews. This even drives some companies to hire independent product reviewers to ensure that there will be accurate reviews of the products. This could help them to spot the improvements that they have to make on their products including their services.

Email Ad's & Marketing Strategies

If you are already into email advertising, most likely you are already aware of the potential that this marketing strategy has to offer. Given this, you are already aware what to expect with it and that you already know that using email marketing alone will not make your business thrive. It is a fact that businesses do not become successful by just focusing on one type of marketing strategy, they have to implore more. It is interesting that email marketing is composed of various strategies. There is the ordinary sending out of emails, online newsletter distribution and online course correspondences. Again, implementing one strategy will not give you great result in traffic and earnings. Thus, you have to implore two or more strategies like using promotional gifts which may provide you with more significant result. It will definitely work to your advantage if you will use other kinds of online promotions for your online business or company.

Some of the techniques that you could use are buying banner ads, space online, starting affiliate programs and participating in forums. Of all of these techniques, banner ads are the most expensive. Online business or online marketing related forums are another strategy that you can use to increase your income by participating in the forum. Online forum is a place online where people share the same interests; they can meet up, discuss things and do other similar tasks. Majority of the online forums allow their members to post links to their websites in their signature line. If you participate in an online business related forums, ensure you include your signature lines. You may link your website to reach your target audience. When you are using online forums to promote your brand awareness, you must follow all forum pointers, avoid strategies that could be considered as spam such as link posting when it is inappropriate. Another helpful promotional tool which can be employed with email marketing is the Affiliate promotional program. In Affiliate advertising, website owners are allowed to post advertisements to the affiliate website. In this set up, website owners are referred to as affiliates. They earn if their advertisements are visited or if there are actual purchase from their site. This compensation strategy makes the affiliate advertising cost effective because you only pay the affiliates based on actual generated traffic or actual purchase of visitors.

To make things clear, the compensation arrangement should be determined before engagement as this is always the case. This could be based on profit sharing or flat rate. In order for the business owners to determine which ads are generating profit, they have to embed a code into the affiliate ads. It is very important to know which affiliates get the attention of the viewers and thus generate them income. They can use this to align the advertising effort of the company to the response of its market.

Huge number of business owners depends on affiliate programs to help their business generate more income. If you are an online business owner, selling a particular product, you may also try affiliate programs and benefit from it. However, it is important to know how to implement it properly. When affiliate programs are properly used, it will greatly increase your revenue without the huge amount of effort on your end. To get started, the first thing is to find the best affiliate tracking software for your online business. So what exactly is affiliate tracking software? It is the actual program behind the affiliate program. It tracks the generated sales which include who made the sales, when the sales were made and what is the amount for the compensation of the affiliates. In affiliate marketing program, sales are usually generated when the banners that you placed in the website of your affiliate are clicked or paid by the visitors. In effect, you have to compensate your affiliate who helped you to make sales.

For the compensation of your affiliates or partners who helped you to generate sales, it is important to account this accurately. This is possible with affiliate tracking software. Thus, if you want to start our own affiliate program, you must have an affiliate tracking software. However, if you are not keen with buying your own, you may ask someone else to use their affiliate tracking software. When you opted to use someone else's affiliate tracking program, you might end up dealing with affiliate networking company. These companies would provide you the tracking software, accounting of the sales made by your affiliates up to sending them the payment. The features of the software that these companies use are unique and better compared to those software that you will buy on your own. Should you decide to buy your own, the software may determine the earnings of all your affiliates but you have to do the other things independently. The problem is can you make out time to do attend to the other pressing issues. Paying your affiliates on a manual basis may work against you because it is more tedious compared to having your own affiliate tracking software. With affiliate tracking software, everything is automated, from the recording of your affiliates to the amount of money that you have to pay them whether it is on a weekly or monthly basis; the whole process becomes easier. This way, you can make use of your time for other things rather than spending more time in calculating the payment for all of your affiliates. It is always better to buy an affiliate tracking software that can provide customer support. Huge numbers of affiliate tracking software programs do not provide this. However, there is still some affiliate tracking software that includes customer service support in their package. In case that the tracking software has a free customer service support, it has to be included in the description of the software features. You have to check it out.

There are some benefits to buying an affiliate tracking software if you decide to buy your own tracking software or to engage a business with affiliate networking company. Whatever your choice will be, it is important to focus on how your choice will increase your profit. Whatever set up you will choose will not directly affect the amount of earnings, rather it will just affect how your program runs.

Belong to More Than One Affiliate Program: Every day, many individuals are earning through affiliate programs such as Commission Junction, Clickbank, Clicksure, Peerfly, MaxBounty, etc… These are usually the webmasters or those who operate their own online business websites. Normally with affiliate programs, there are many people who want to earn more. The good thing about affiliate program is that you can join more than one program which could help you earn more. However, joining many affiliate programs could be very confusing and may rather be a step backward for you. If you are really interested in joining multiple affiliate programs then it is important to learn how to handle this properly. The main problem with joining many affiliate programs is that you will have a hard time tracking your earnings compared to having a single affiliate program. However, you can optimize this in a way that it will work best for you. This could be more confusing and time consuming. Thus, the more affiliate program you join, the more earnings but the more difficulty in tracking your earnings if not well organized by you.

The first option for some people when tracking their earnings from the multiple affiliate programs is that they want to track it manually, by the use of pen and paper. However, there is an affiliate tracking software that could make the tracking of all your earnings done automatically. Therefore, if you are really keen to join many affiliate marketing programs and earn more money, then this is the best solution to your problem.

When you want to buy an affiliate software program, you have to check that it is compatible with the various affiliate programs that you joined. This is because many affiliate programs managed through third party programs such as Link Share, Clickbank and other similar programs have their own tracking software. If you are not a member of their programs then, it is necessary for you to find other tracking software. Clickbank is a very good place to start and I will encourage you to consider joining them as they cover many niches. If you are interested in obtaining affiliate tracking software, you will have a number of different options. There are a number of software programs that you can obtain free, but others are not. The best way to decide on affiliate tracking software is to examine all of your available options. This can easily be done by performing a standard internet search. Simply by performing a search with the words, affiliate tracking software, you should be provided with a number of different results. Those results should include software programs that are obtainable for a small fee or free to use. Just choose the one that is best suited for your needs. However, I have included a list of many of these 'underground websites' that you can visit on chapter 7 of this book. From the results of your search, you will see that many affiliate software programs are the same. All of them have single aim and that is to make the tracking and processing of your earnings easier such as generating click reports, financial reports and pending pay-out records. Even though almost all of them have the same features, it is still advisable to examine all its features to know whether they are suitable for your needs or not.

As an online entrepreneur, your properly managed affiliate program could provide you with increase in sales. Through this software, it will become easy for you to reward your affiliates for the work well done which could motivate them to perform better. Thus, if you will go into affiliate program then it is necessary that you have to source for the right affiliate software tracking system. The greatest advantage of buying the most recommended affiliate tracking software is that it serves online business owners well. From there, you would know which of the software you have to avoid especially if they have negative reviews.

Generally, people provide negative reviews for certain products to ensure that no one will fall trap to poor performing products though at times some reviews could be malicious especially where there are many competition. On the other hand, when people provide their recommendations, this means that they want other people to experience the benefits that they have experienced. If a software program is highly recommended, then it is most likely the people who recommended it are still using the product and you can get in touch with them. You may connect with them and ask some tips on how you can make the most out of such tracking software.

Chapter 9
Improving and Focusing on Other Ways to Promote Your Business

<u>In This Chapter</u>

Creating Your Sales Page

Email Marketing

Coupon Offers

Free Advertising

Setting Up Auto Responders and Using Squeeze Pages

Exploring New Marketing Technique

Rekindling Customer Relations Through Feedbacks, Reviews, Surveys, etc

Creating Your Sales Page

A good sales page is like a search engine optimization with good 'Call to Action'. Search Engine Optimization (SEO) efforts could take a long time to produce results because doing SEO is a continuous work. Given this, you must have the diligence and the patience in order for you to achieve success in doing SEO. The most frustrating part though is that when you have exerted so much effort and have given all the patience and yet there was no increase in traffic or in sales. In order for you to avoid such frustration, you have to ensure that your website present a clear message that drives people to action. From the onset, you have to make it clear that the purpose of your website is to generate sales. However, you should not do this blatantly on your website. You just have to make it obvious for viewers that you have some products for sale. Highlight the hot deals and the freebies that the client will get if they order online. Also, emphasize how easy and secure your order process is. Another way to call their attention to act is by providing the viewers the chance to connect with you on a regular basis. Make yourself reachable to your customers by making it easy for them to access your RSS feed, email or newsletter. You can try creating an online group and have the prospective members sign up. When they sign up, you have to make some attractive offers to them so that they will get back to you often.

Lastly, be creative. You can think of other activities that could encourage the viewers to buy every time that they visit your website. The more effort you make to get people to visit your site, the more results you will get in your SEO results.

Email Marketing

It is commonly known that email marketing is one of the best strategies to use and tap into new clients. With email marketing you can communicate directly to your clients and expand your business. However, for those who have not used email before, this statement seems somewhat vague that it would prompt them to ask for more clarification. There are four main questions that people usually ask regarding email marketing in order for them to fully understand its concept.

What is an email marketing: Email marketing is a "direct" means of marketing that uses email to reach clients or target market without the need of any third parties such as radio, television etc…

In order for businesses to get started with email marketing, they have to secure the contact details of their prospective customers. These prospective customers must have shown real interests with the products and services that you are offering. Once you have the list of their contact details, you can send them emails regarding the products or services that they are interested in.

Why email marketing is worth it: Email marketing is worth your time and effort because it has been proven to be an effective tool in marketing. It enables you to directly get in touch with your prospective clients and inform them about the products and services that they are interested in. Also, it will be possible to establish solid business relationship with your prospective clients by sending them an email newsletter. This strategy generates high traffic and earnings.

Is Email Marketing a Form of Spamming: Many are quite hesitant to do email marketing because they see it somewhat like "spamming". In effect, they are afraid that they might send away prospective clients instead of attracting them. This could happen only if done incorrectly. Prioritize sending emails to those who have shown keen interest to your products and you will see the great result.

Ways to Ensure That Your Email Marketing is Effective: Email marketing is all about numbers and creating value. So if you want to ensure effective result in email marketing you must have quality list of prospective clients. They could be regular readers of your blog or those people who are already in your email contact list. Bear I mind that these people must have keen interest in whatever products or services that you are offering. The more quality lists that you have the more effective result you will get. Email marketing can be your most effective marketing tool or could be the big waste of your resources. This largely depends on how you use it. If you have done due diligence by knowing you target market, getting their contacts and ensuring that your email will not go to their spam folders, then you will achieve a good result. If you sent emails in an improper manner, they might end up in their Spam folders and therefore unread by them.

Watch Out for the Spam Words: There are words that are usually used by Spammers, so don't use them. There are huge list of words that you should avoid using such as discount, free, bonus, guarantee etc... Also, do not use all caps in the subject lines and avoid exclamation marks.

Update Your Lists: Make sure to update your list. Do not send messages to emails that bounced back because the email is wrong or no longer active as you might be marked as a Spammer. Also remove in your list those who have not shown interest to your offers for a long time. This will improve the effectiveness of your email marketing and lessen the possibility of sending emails to your prospective clients' spam folders.

Remove Non-subscribers Immediately: Remove immediately from your list those who unsubscribed. This will save you from being marked as a Spammer. You have to be quick with this as people are also quick to decide when they do not want something.

Do Email Testing: Do an email testing to various major email providers such as Yahoo, Gmail and Hotmail before you send out actual emails to your prospective clients.

This is to ensure that the emails that you will send them will not go to their Spam Folders. If the result of your testing is good then you can continue with emailing.

Coupon Offers

Don't Forget Your Coupon Offers: The common mistake that online business owners make is of not offering their prospective clients online-shopping coupon. You have to remember that online shoppers are looking for the best deals around. Thus, offering them coupon discounts will make it easier for you to set your foot on their entrance doors.

Even if you have done all your homework to hit the ground running for your online business, it will not produce great results if you have failed to give your targeted market coupon offers.

Here are some tips on how to give your prospective clients their coupon offers.

Decide the Amount of Discount and What Offer You Will Give: If you are selling products that will generate you high income, you can consider providing 20% off coupon on your actual price. If you are shipping products and the shipment fee is somewhat expensive, you might try giving free shipment or discounted shipment fee so that your prospective clients will be encouraged to order.

You have to study carefully though what kind of discount rates you will provide, make sure that your earnings will not be sacrificed as well.

Decide Who Qualifies for the Discount Offer: You may also try to give discount offers on per order basis. For cheaper products you may give discount for buying with the minimum amount of $100 as an example.

Identify the Duration of Your Offer: Definitely, your offer cannot go on forever. Thus, it is important to know the specific duration of your discounts. Also, discount offers that do not have deadline do not give the sense of urgency for people to grab your offer. Make your clients buy your services or products today. When you have already set the duration of your discount offer, make sure that you communicate this to your customers to avoid frustrating your clients.

Know How to Distribute Your Online Coupon: You have to ensure that your discount offer will be known to your clients. You can add them to your social media account or to your blog. A good option is to combine it with your affiliate network. This will attract people who are willing to promote your products or services online. You just have to give them commission. This strategy is a solid one that can get the response of large number of people.

Apart from these methods, there are other ways to use and promote your discount coupons. You just have to study carefully on how you are going to make it. Also, do not be afraid to experiment and come up with new ideas.

Free Advertising

When you have a website, it is important to generate huge traffic as fast as you can. You can achieve this by using advertisement. The common notion is that advertising is expensive but this is not always the case. There are many ways to use and get free advertisement that could be effective, you just have to be both resourceful and creative. So money is not always a starting point for an advertisement. When we talk about free advertisement, the most effective and free to use is the internet provided that you know how to go around it properly.

These Are the Five Tips on How to Make a Free Advertisement Online:

Use Your Email as an Advertising Tool: Many are not aware that they could use their own email as a good marketing tool. Whenever you send out an email, make sure that you have a professional signature at the end of your email. In your email signature, you must include your website or the tag line of your business which will give the recipients some ideas about the services that you are offering. This would help to generate traffic to your website and could help you to have additional sales.

Ask People to Refer Their Friends: Referral is one of the most effective marketing tools. This is because when a friend refers a product to another friend, the latter usually trusts that such product is reliable and will like to try it. If the product is good they will spread the word and you will have increased sales. There are different ways for referral; you may include a "refer a friend" button to your website, use social networking sites to build your network or to provide incentives to those who will refer. You can never go wrong with the power of the word of mouth.

Maximize the Use of SEO: SEO is a very reliable tool in advertisement as millions of people are searching something over the internet every day. When you implore SEO to your website provided that you are good, it will land on the top pages in search engines. Therefore, when people are searching for services, they will easily see your website and what you are offering. So, you have to use what you have already learnt about SEO and study the other things that you still don't know and benefit from it. This free advertisement could make you capture big market from all over the globe.

Post Your Services on Free Classifieds: Check out the popular free classifieds which are widely used and viewed by people and advertise your services there. Make your advertisement enticing and stand out so that the viewers will notice you. This free advertising is tested to give you the desired result.

Get into Discussion Forums: In discussion forums, there are various groups of people. You can select your target market and join the discussion group. However, you have to be creative in advertising your services as hard core advertisement is not allowed there. The key here is to be subtle, so that you would not sound like you are really advertising or marketing. The good thing about forums is that you can go directly to your target market plus the number of members grows as time passes by.

People could make earning money online complicated when it is just very simple. The most important thing that you have to remember is that making money online is all about best strategies to use in generating huge traffic by spending little or nothing at all. Again, this is because traffic means income. These are the two things that you have to remember with free online advertising:

Use of Interaction in Advertising: There are various avenues you can use to interact online such as <u>forums</u>, social networking sites like <u>Twitter,</u> <u>Facebook</u>, <u>YouTube</u>, <u>LinkedIn</u>, <u>Pinterest</u>, <u>SlideShare</u>, <u>Google +</u> etc. You can leave comments on their walls or pages, Twitter posts, retweets, LinkedIn groups, or post comments to their blogs and yours. You have to make effort to be reachable by your target market. Let them be able to follow you on all these networks and you can also join open networks on LinkedIn that are for your target market. This strategy will give you more traffic to your website. The good thing is that you can link most of these networks so that one post you send out goes to the rest. You just need to learn how to do this.

Search engines such as Google, Bing, AOL and Yahoo are also ad Forums: The search engines are reliable tools for advertisement. When people are searching for almost anything, they rely on the search engines to find the answers. People also do ask questions on these search forums and providing answers to those questions without misusing the system will also generate traffic to your website especially when you leave a link pointing back to a solution that is relevant to the question asked.

Affordable Advertising: There are many ways to do advertising for a lesser fee. This includes Pay Per Click (PPC), promotions and offering special deals. PPC is a way to advertise online without spending big amount of money if you do not wish to. You will drive visitors to your website when they click your link. As for offering promotions or special deals, you will spend some money but the response of the people is immediate and it totally gives traffic to your websites. It encourages new visitors to see your website and your offers.

Setting Up Auto Responders and Using Squeeze Pages

If you have a squeeze (Opt in) page with an attractive free offer and you failed to secure leads that could generate income, then the problem could be with your offer or the landing page or the origin of the traffic. All these have to be properly configured and optimized as they are all important for generating traffic to your website. Attracting good visitors to your website is not that complicated if these excellent strategies are applied correctly.

Use of URL Rotator Script: It is very important that you as a smart online business owner or online marketer is always checking your websites to see how you can improve yours SEO and website performance. You can achieve this by carrying out landing page split test through a URL rotator script. The rotator script will display 2 different versions of the identical page.

This will also help you to know exactly how your landing page is performing. You can also URL Rotator script for rotating multiple affiliate links to enable exchange of traffic between your affiliate links. This will also enable you to keep track of the number of clicks on your websites. It is highly recommended that websites change headlines on a regular basis because it will help to maximize your optimization and thus improve conversions. URL Rotator also allows you to randomize the traffic that goes to your online businesses especially where it is difficult to promote all individually.

Sign Up Forms Should Be Eye Catchy: The sign up form or landing page where people will fill out their information must be attractive to the eyes. This could be a simple and yet elegant buttons or forms. You can be more creative with your presentation by using texts or videos to convey your message. You can include unique images or texts to the forms. It must stand out and could offer value to your website visitors given that you also have other online competitors.

Exploring New Marketing Strategies

Understanding Video Marketing: The rule of thumb in creating a good video is to write good articles. This is because the articles that you write will be used to make the videos. In order for you to come up with a good article, it has to be relevant with the services that you are offering and it has to be timely. Your articles must capture the interest of the people at the current time. Also, you have to use SEO friendly keywords for your articles. With this, you have to check out Google keyword tools to see what the keywords that you must use are. When you already have a good article then you can create the video. There are so many tools available for you to choose from including free video creation tool. Some of these tools you can find on your Bonus 2 at the end of this book. Make sure that the color and background of your video is pleasing to the viewers. Check the texts that you will put in the video to make sure that it will look good on the video. In case that you want to make some improvements, you can change them anytime. Then try to record the video personally, from there you will see whether it is good or would need more improvements. Do this until you achieve the most effective video marketing you want. Even if you create a simple video, you will still get results however making the best video will give you the best result. It's your choice.

Rekindling Customer Relationship through Feedback, Reviews, Surveys, etc

You can always rekindle customer relationship by designing surveys for getting customer feedbacks. This job is not really difficult. However, it will require enough time for planning. You need to be creative with questions that your target audience would love to answer.

Laying The Groundwork: Before you start creating your questionnaire, you should first gather all necessary information from reliable resources. You should never forget to involve your target audience in your project. In that way, you can encourage them to cooperate with you.

Development and Launch: Once you are done with gathering all necessary information, the next thing that you should do is to begin working on the design of your survey. Your questionnaire should only focus on a single service, product, or brand. In that way, you will get full value from the answers of your respondents. It is very important that you offer them incentive to enable them to fill the form for you. Do not make your questionnaire long. Keep it short and simple so that your respondents will not find it boring to answer. Before sending your survey to your respondents, you should first make a follow-up plan wherein your employees will answer any complaints from your customers. These employees may or may not be involved in your surveying team. Do not forget to notify your key personnel. In that way, you will get their full support throughout the process.

Data Collection and Analysis: Once you have deployed your customer opinion questionnaire, the next thing that you should do is to perform some preliminary analysis of the results. This step will help you in identifying all recurring complaints that need your quick response. As you collect all of your respondents' responses, you should review your plan and follow up with them.

Taking Action: Analyzing survey results might be time consuming. You can just use an application or software that will automate the analysis for you. It will not only help you save time, but it will also keep all analysis accurate. Conducting regular surveys is a very effective way of getting feedback and comments from your customers. It will contribute a lot in the growth and development of your products and company.

Chapter 10
Facebook For Business

In This Chapter

Why Your Online Business Needs Facebook

Designing a Stunning, Customized Facebook Fan Page

Why You Cannot Afford Not to Offer Discounts or Deals

Online Business and Facebook Advertising

Utilize a Fan Page to Your Benefit

Tools That Can Help Drive Sales to Your Online Business

Optimizing Your Online Business for Facebook Customers

Build Partnerships with Other Pages

Using Social Plugins and Badges

Why Your Online Business Needs Facebook

If you have just started your online business, you should consider using Facebook to make it become more popular, especially to your target audience. Facebook has over half billion of members. It also generates lots of traffic. Many people have a Facebook account so you will surely find your target audience there.

If you have a Facebook account, you may have noticed the advertisement that popup on the right hand corner of the page every time you browse the site. Those advertisements are constantly changing depending on the interests of the person who owns the account. You can use Facebook ads to make your business popular. You have a huge chance to make much money by just targeting Facebook users that might be interested to your products.

Facebook allows you to share videos or affiliate links by posting them. You may share your blogs and articles so that your target readers will learn more about you as well as the business that you are currently running.

Designing a Stunning, Customized Facebook Fan Page

A customized Facebook fan page provides a very wide range of business solutions that can increase the possibility of developing a stable business community as well as a huge client base. You may also create your own Facebook application that will boost or generate leads to your business. If you do not have time in creating and maintaining your Facebook fan page and applications, you may outsource it. There are already companies that collaborate with small businesses to help generate sales by using Facebook marketing.

Here are the Facebook changes you should know about:

The Facebook Timeline - The Story of Your Life: Timeline is the most visible change on Facebook. It also serves as your business' Facebook profile. It looks really organized, so you need to maximize its use. You can post your profile picture or your business' logo there. You may also post a cover photo at the top that will serve as your banner. The Facebook Timeline is the profile page of your business. You can list all your services there as well as the significant dates or events that are really valuable to your business.

Open Graph Features: Facebook now has open graph features that help you track all the activities on your timeline. The biggest part of these features is the way it allows you to interact with other types of media. Applications will no longer ask for your permission repeatedly. The new Facebook permission screen will just explain the types of stories that will be shared every time you give application permission to your post.

Facebook has already divided updates into 2 different categories – posts and activities. All posts show up in the newsfeed, while all activities show up in the ticker.

These activities have four main categories which include communication, media, games, and lifestyle.

Yahoo News and Other News Websites: Once you opt in to this service, you will see the news stories that your friends or contacts are reading.

Spotify: Once you opt in to this service, you will discover more music through your Facebook friends. You will be able to see who's currently listening to a song and once you hover over the ticker, you will also be able to listen to that song.

The Like Button: The Like Button is used to like a brand, product, company, or person. Apart from this button, there are also some other available options to choose from.

Email Notifications: Facebook no longer sends e-mail notifications for every update on your page. You will only receive important notifications like the summary of the stories that you have missed and reports about your lifestyle applications. Any email you receive from Facebook goes into your Facebook messages for you to read.

What Shows Up in News Feeds: Your Facebook newsfeed just ranks the top stories and latest updates on your page. Facebook has already added a control at the top right part of each story so the users can check to mark and unmark the top story. As you can see, you now have more control over your news feeds. You can also choose to view either the top stories or latest updates.

What's Next: We recommend you to start making strategic plans for your business' Facebook page. These recent changes are quite huge, but they are really good and useful especially for business owners like you.

Offering Discounts or Deals: People love to receive deals or get discounts. You can attract more people to visit your website by simply offering discounts and deals that they can use to buy your products in more affordable prices.

Facebook Advertising: If you want to use the advertising services of Facebook, you need to pay some amount of money to get started. There are 2 types of payment for advertising on Facebook. The first one is called CPC and the other one is called CTR.

Cost Per Click (CPC): It is the amount of clicks the advertisement receives or the number of times your ad is shown in the Facebook page. CPC is the same as PPC or "pay per click."

Click Through Rate (CTR): Also known as CPM or "cost per thousand impressions") is used for brand awareness. This is an advertisement that leads into actual conversions of ad impressions. CPM is charged per impression even without any click on the advertisement.

Here are the Actual Advertising Prices for Each Advertising Option on Facebook:

For CPC bid, your budget depends on how much you are willing to spend on a particular day.

For CTR bid, the default rate is $25, but you can change it to $1 if you like. Once you have already added your new campaign, complete the transaction by selecting the type of bid that you want to take. After that, decide on the schedule of your advertisement. Facebook advertising has no hidden charges, so you will only pay for what you set on the bid.

Online Business and Facebook Advertising

Advertising is one of the most important processes that a business should undergo. Online Business entrepreneurs need to ensure that their target audiences are aware that the company exists in order for them to generate sales. Advertising is the process of attracting your target audience to try out your products. Not all companies that advertise their products become successful. You need to think of a great advertising strategy in order for you to stand out in the market.

Previously, advertising was only done on television, radio, billboards, flyers, brochures, posters, and newspapers. Now, it can also be done on the Internet. You may use social media, like Facebook and Twitter, to get more customers. You may also create a blog where you are going to post updates about your business. Of course, your online ads should always point back to your main website.

Advertising on Facebook: Advertising for small companies is easy with Facebook. Facebook advertising is really affordable. In fact, it is almost free. You just need to know the best ways to do advertising on Facebook. You may advertise on your fan page. You may also advertise by buying Facebook ads.

When advertising on Facebook, the first thing that you need to do is to read the Frequently Asked Questions (FAQs) page of the website. It will help you learn more about the site as well as the best ways to advertise your product or brand. You will also find the answers to all of your questions on that page.

Once you have familiarized yourself with the guidelines, you may now move on to choose your target audience. Facebook allows you to choose the people whom your advertisements will be shown to. They will be the place to do the work of targeting your audience. You just need to tell Facebook more about the types of people that you want to advertise your product or brand to. You may specify the country, city, age, interests, gender, hobbies, or occupation of the people that you want to target. These factors are called "demographics."

After that, you can start creating your ads right away. Facebook encourages adverts with photos and text elements when creating the ads. Once you are done with creating your ad campaign, it is now time for you to select the types of ads that you want to post. You may choose CPC or CPM. After that, you just need to start your ads!

Facebook Conversion Tracking Pixel: Facebook recently introduced the new Conversion Pixel which is aimed at helping businesses to measure return on their investment based on use of Facebook ads. This conversion pixel is capable of reporting actions people take after viewing your ads on Facebook. To achieve this, you will first need to set it up through your Facebook adverts link on your page. You will need to specify the type of tracking you want to report e.g. leads, sales, checkout etc and all you have to do is to place the script in between the 'Head' section on your website where you want the tracking to be done. Then the script will track it back to Facebook ads therefore enabling your online business to enjoy more conversion.

This track conversion pixel is capable of tracking your customer behavior between 1-28 days of viewing your ads or clicking on your ads on Facebook. To learn more visit Facebook Conversion Tracking Help page . To learn more on how to create an ad or sponsored story on Facebook, visit Facebook ads help page and Facebook for Business page.

Facebook Graph Search: Facebook recently introduced the Graph Search which will make it easier for friends and connections to find out about other people's interest on Facebook and therefore connect with the right people. The search will be unique to you as a person based on your friends and connections. This will definitely be a great tool for businesses when it is eventually launched as Facebook is only trialing it at the moment.

Utilize a Fan Page to Your Benefit

Facebook is now one of the leading sites where companies can market their products. If you want to get more customers from Facebook, you need to maximize its usage. You need to create an engaging fan page for your online business.

Custom Tabs: Facebook allows you to create custom ads. If you want your page to stand out, you need to customize your tabs in a way that your readers will find it easy to navigate.

Using an Exhibit Page: If you want to attract more clients, you should use an exhibit page where you can post special offers that will catch the interest of your Facebook followers.

Update Your Facebook with Your Latest Blog Post: Every time you update your blog, do not forget to post the link to your latest blog entry on your Facebook page. Also, make sure that your blog post contains a link to your website.

In that way, you can easily generate traffic to your blog and website at the same time.

Here is a Checklist That You can Use as a Guide in Creating a Great Facebook Page:

Create your Facebook page from scratch

Give your page a unique name..Example. http://www.facebook.com/GoldVenturesLtd

Monetize your page by using a landing page or welcome page or sales page

Add content to your page (videos, texts, photos)

Get direct traffic to your page through outsourcing

Try to use Direct Hubs for business

Create an Auto responder

Integrate your online store to your Facebook page

Optimizing Your Online Business for Facebook Customers

There are 20 easy steps that will enable your business to engage more with your Facebook customers for better return on investment which will lead you towards making money online while you sleep.

- Fill out your Facebook profile completely
- Create a Facebook page that you will use for business
- Read Facebook rules for creating business accounts
- Set the privacy setting of your page
- Set up a separate friends lists for friends and business
- Click the "boxes" tab and add your videos
- Post your newsletters or press releases on your Facebook business page
- Obtain a vanity URL for your Facebook page.
- Do not forget to add your Facebook URL to all of your marketing stuff (leaflets, business cards, letters, etc.)
- Post updates of your business to your page
- Share only valuable content to your page
- Create accounts on Twitter and LinkedIn and other social media and link them to your Facebook page
- Read the profiles of your followers and search for your potential clients
- Engage with your contacts and invite them to like your page & connect with them

- Share posts with your followers and people who are working in the same industry as yours

- Promote discounts, offers, coupons, contests of your products or service

- Make sure to share your website links on your Facebook page

- Boost your presence using Facebook ads and PPC. Keep your followers updated with your upcoming events

- Post some other interesting stuff and do not just use your Facebook page only for selling purposes but interact as well.

Build Partnerships with Other Pages

By setting up your own Facebook page, you will have the chance to get joint venture relationships with other small businesses. You may build a long-term working relationship with other companies that can help in making your business popular on the internet. You may share links with them, too.

Facebook Marketing Partnership: It is a bit easy to generate traffic using targeted demographics though the hard work is with the conversion. However, you may deal with other small businesses that already have established Facebook pages. In this way, they will be able to help you get more presence online. This partnership will help you save money by not hiring a full-time social media professional.

Content for Page: You always need to be creative when creating content for your Facebook page. You may use eye-catching photos that will encourage your readers to read your posts. You may also post videos if you want and ask questions that can trigger answers. There is nothing wrong with posting texts only, but it might bore your readers. You need to make your posts diverse.

Give Back to the Fan Community: Never ever forget to give back to your fans or Facebook followers. Without them, your business will never grow. In this case, you may give them some rewards occasionally. You may also send some discount coupons to them from time to time. If you ask them to help in generating leads to your site, you may give them some revenue share as well.

Using Social Plugins and Badges

Wordpress plugins and Twitter tools are helpful in getting more benefit from your blog. They can help you in increasing your popularity and visibility online.

Here are the recommended Wordpress Plugins that You can Use to Add Twitter Plugins on Your Blog:

- AddToAny
- Add Twitter RSS
- Feed2Tweet
- FishyTweet
- TwiBadge & MyTwitpic

If you are looking for some Twitter tools that will help you connect with your clients and gain more popularity online, you may simply use NewsTweet, Feed2Tweet, FishyTweet, and Twibadge.

Chapter 11
Ten Steps To Becoming a Successful Online Entrepreneur

In This Chapter

Be Passionate About What You Do

Invest in Your Education and Learning

Create a Focused, Achievable Business and Marketing Plans

Even the Biggest Online Businesses are Always Looking for Clients

Endeavor to Reinvent Your Product and Yourself

Think Success Always and Pick Yourself up Even if You Fail

Integrity is the Watch Word.

Do Not Promise What You Cannot Deliver

Join Likeminded Networks and Surround Yourself with Great Master Mind Team

Relax and Have Fun

Be Passionate About What You Do

Most people have the same excuse when it comes to thinking of a new business idea. They usually say that they need more time to come up with a great business idea. They are not aware that it is a very common fallacy. You do not need much time just to start a soon-to-be successful online business.

If you are still planning to start an online business, you should understand that time does not matter the most but what matters is the way you use your time in building your business. Some successful online business owners only spend an hour or two a day in managing their business. So, you only need to work smart and not hard.

Believe it or not, spending an hour a day for your online business will surely produce greater achievements than working for lots of hours. You will not only have much time to rest, but also more time for your family and other important matters. How can you manage to spend an hour a day for work? The answer to this question is very simple. Just follow your plan. If you do not have any plans yet, then you need to make one now.

Do not spend too much time in creating your plan. Here is a plan that I recommend to you. This plan will focus on the 3 core areas of your daily business – list, traffic, products or services. Just focus on these areas consistently and you will surely maintain balance in your business. These are also considered as the fundamentals or basics of your success in the online business industry.

You need to develop a great way of working by spending time on the said targets. These targets will serve as the foundation of your online marketing business. Always keep in mind that if your business does not have any foundation, it will never be stable. Of course, everybody wants to have a stable business. In this case, you need to take time in creating a regular work plan.

First, you need to organize your whole work week by creating a schedule of your daily activities. You may use a planner or a notebook for this. You may also organize your schedules using your computer. Just make a Google search for the best Weekly Planners online. Make sure that your planner covers your morning, afternoon, and evening schedules. If you are naturally a disorganized person, then you just need to always think of the importance of the success of your online business. In that way, you will become motivated to come up with a simple discipline in creating a weekly schedule that will bring huge improvement in your work productivity.

You should always be realistic when it comes to filling up and completing your weekly schedule. Take note that your business should only involve enjoyable and exciting processes and not just chores. You should not just schedule your work hours. You also need to schedule your non-working hours. These are the hours that you spend with your family, for your regular exercise, for watching TV, or whatever hobby that you love to do on a daily basis. You do not need to spend all of your time at work. You need to have a balanced life. In that way, you will be able to make your schedule sustainable all the time. If you are a family man or woman and you have a full-time job, your schedule might be already full at the moment. However, there are some ways on how you can find an extra hour to spend for a very exciting and profitable project. Good time management is the key here.

Once you have already established your working and non-working schedules, it is now time for you to determine the things that you want to achieve on the 3 core areas of your business (list, traffic, and products or services). However, you should not just list down everything that comes to your mind. You need to break down every big task into smaller and manageable tasks. Why do you need to do this? This strategy will help you in becoming more productive. You will be able to finish the tasks little by little.

If you are not able to finish everything that you have scheduled during the previous working days, you may do them on the last day of your work week. During the last work week, you should also schedule the things that you are planning to do next week. The process of scheduling is quite repetitive, so you will surely get used to it as time goes by. Just stick to your schedules and you will be fine.

Invest In Your Education and Learning

Online millionaires spend their time and money to get further education about the latest trends in online business. You need to enroll to online classes that will help you learn all the business strategies online today that will enable you to come up with your own ideas and products. Education is still a very good investment even in building up a new online business. Never be afraid of making mistakes while learning because, there is always room for improvement, and many have failed but were determined to rise above their failure.

Online Millionaires are Not All Made Overnight: If you have already attended some Internet marketing seminars, you have surely noticed that all of them feature online marketing gurus who shared their personal tips on how to succeed in online business. You may have also noticed that their stories are similar. You know, those gurus do not really reveal the whole real road to their success. They do not always share their fears and losses to aspiring online business owners.

It do take some online millionaires an average of 6 months to 6 years to get their first million from online sales. As long as you know what you are doing and can lay down a strategy for generating converting leads, you too could reach that level but you must discipline yourself by being focused on a specific plan. Hence, I would like to challenge you to apply all the strategies that you have been taught in this book and see if you cannot make millions like other online business owners.

Online Millionaires are Not Necessarily Idle: Many of us picture a typical successful online business owner as beach lovers who just go online from time to time to check their online sales, but they are not! Well, some of them may be. Those online millionaires could be called anytime, even in the early hours of the day because they are still wide awake and working strong.

Outsourcing for Online Millionaires: Some people think that online millionaires do all the tasks on their own or just hire other people to do every necessary job for them. Take note that online millionaires are hustlers when it comes to implementing Internet processes. They know that there is an exact sequence in doing online business and they just stick to it. They just get as many people as possible to sell their products and services to.

Online millionaires know what they are really good at and what they need other people for. They only hire the right people to do very specific and targeted tasks. Not all online millionaires are great web designers. Some of them do not even know how to setup their own shopping cart. However, they know exactly how to control everything and in what sequence.

Do Online Millionaires Turn Everything They Touch into Gold: Online millionaires are successful than others but not because of magic. There is something more than just a magic touch and that is "patience." Online gurus take time to test everything. They constantly check and update the content of their sites, they monitor the activities of their readers, they put efforts in building traffic, they check results from time and time, and they just make more necessary changes. Testing is a very time-consuming job, and not everyone has the patience to wait for their desired results.

Do Online Millionaires Love Writing? If you think that online millionaires are born writers, then you are wrong. In fact, more than half of all online millionaires hate writing. However, they found some ways on how to communicate with their potential buyers like using audio or video materials or hiring someone to do the writing job for them.

Why is writing Very Important in Internet Marketing? Well, writing is always the simplest and least expensive way to attract people to check out your products or services. If you hate writing or you think that you just do not have great writing skills, then you should work towards knowing how it is done. Determination and willingness to learn always pay off.

Online Millionaires Offer Just One Product or One Service: Some people think that every online millionaire only focuses on offering a solitary product. They are wrong. Most online millionaires sell 10 or more products and services that are being offered by other people. Always keep in mind that if you will just focus on selling your own products and services, you will surely taking the long road to the millionaire status.

Create a Focused, Achievable Business and Marketing Plans

Whether your business focuses on monetized blogging or selling your own products and services, here are the 10 key qualities that you must possess to achieve online business success.

You: Your business will never become stable and successful without you. So, you need to possess the entrepreneurial spirit, the determination and the will to become successful.

The Money Opportunity: In order for you to make much money online, you need to find the right way on how to do it. You need to determine the right medium in order for you to generate streams of income using the Internet. Leverage the power of affiliate marketing.

Your Offer: Once you have discovered the money opportunity that suits you, you need to determine what you can offer to take advantage on that opportunity. You need to come up with an idea that will make your target audience choose your offer over other existing offers online.

Advertising: Once you have successfully decided on the product or service that you are going to offer to your target audience, the next step that you need to do is advertise it. You need to put effort in making your business more visible in the online world in order for you to get more customers.

Allowing Growth: Once you have started generating sales online, you should come up with an idea on how to maintain the flow of sales.

Achieving Results: Once you start getting your desired results, you should determine which of your marketing strategies do not really work. Eliminate errors and start searching for more strategies that will help your business grow.

Recruiting Plans: As your business grows, you will need help from other people in handling and maintaining it. If you are a blogger, you might need to hire more bloggers to help you with the writing and advertising tasks. Of course, you need to pay them as well.

Product Development: Your product needs to be developed based on the ever-changing needs of your target customers. You need to think of some things that will make your product become more powerful in the market.

Customer Service: Every business should have great customer service. You should always desire to get positive feedback and comments from your clients. You should always take time to answer all of your clients' questions and inquiries soon. You should not just focus on getting new customers.

You should also focus on keeping them. In that way, you will be able to build long-term business relationship with them.

Enjoy Your Work: Once you have successfully setup your business and started generating money from it, it is now the time for you to enjoy it. You may reward yourself with anything you want.

Apply These Tips to Your Online Business Plan: An online business may be appealing, but it can also be intimidating at the same time. You might ask yourself many times about the right steps to take. Do not worry because here are the tips that will help you in starting your own online business plan.

There are thousands of online business owners who communicate with each other online. Check out some online communities or forums where you can find online marketers that you can connect with. Of course, you need to connect to those business owners who are working in the same niche as yours. Ask them for some tips and advice.

It is also important for you to make sure that your online business goes well with the schedule of your entire family because you might need their help from time to time as well.

You should also take note of all of your transactions. Keep in mind that your current tax situation might change once you become a business owner. Register your online business if you have not done so yet.

If you want to become a successful online business owner, you need to work as professionally as you can. You need to have a professional website that will attract your

customers to buy your products and services. You may visit the websites of similar businesses to get some website design ideas.

If you have a full-time job, you should not give it up yet. It is not ideal to quit your main source of income just to focus on your other job. Keep your old job while your business is still new. Once your business starts growing and you can see there is a regular cash flow that is able to replace your income, you can then quit your job and focus on it, but it might take few years for your online business to become profitable though this is dependent on how fast you can move forward by leveraging the opportunities you have been exposed to in this book.

Always keep track of the prices that your competitors offer. You need to come up with competitive prices that will never be refused by your target clients. However, you should not charge lower than the average market rates if you do not want to get lower profit.

Never ever provide any of your services without a contract. You need to create contracts that will lay out everything that the involved parties must do or not do to prevent any misunderstandings or disagreements.

Every time your business makes profit, you need to keep record of it so that you will be able to save money for your yearly taxes. Always pay yourself salary first if your online business replaces your income.

Find a perfect spot in your house or flat and use it as your permanent work place. You need to keep it clean and organized always. You need to keep things in order so that you will always be determined to work.

Your home based online business should always be based on a detailed and comprehensive plan. It may change over time, but you need to consider it as your to-do list where you can always check your business paths and goals.

All contracts should be kept in a secured place. Of course, you also need to keep them in a place that you can easily find them. You need to keep them handy all the time in case unpredictable circumstances happen between you and your business partners.

Financial business planning is a very important part of building a home based online business. You need to prepare a projected income statement all the time. You also need to break down your projected expenses, sales, and profits. You also need to deposit money to the bank when you get some profits or automate it directly to your bank account or through PayPal depending on the product and the payment system in use. Always deposit checks (cheques) soon to prevent them from getting lost.

Create a banner page for your business website. In that way, you will be able to build a banner exchange program with your business partners. This method is effective in increasing your website's search ranking.

Another important thing that you need to keep in mind is to separate your business e-mails from your personal e-mails. Create a business e-mail address that uses your website's domain name. Give it to your clients so that all of your business related e-mails will go there.

It is also recommended for you to join discussion groups and forums that focus on the online business topics. In that way, you will be able to connect with other online business owners and get some new ideas from them. You may also share your ideas to them in return. This strategy will help you build an online reputation for your business.

There may be times when you need to borrow money from investors to maintain your business. In this case, you need to be ready for all the questions that they may ask before lending you the money. Take note that investors ask questions that you both like and do not like to answer.

Whenever your product gets out of stock, you need to inform your clients soon. In that way, you will never upset them. Hope you learned some important things from these tips. Make sure to apply them to make your online business become successful.

Even the Biggest Online Businesses are Always Looking for Clients.

Yes, because that's how they make their cash flow endless.

Endeavor to Re-invent Your Product and Yourself

Change is the only thing constant. When you see opportunities or changes that should be of benefit to your online business, it is very important that you embrace such opportunities to continue succeeding.

Think Success Always and Pick Yourself Up Even if You Fail

Even the biggest businesses and wealthiest entrepreneurs do fail. However, what is more important is what you can do when you have fallen. It is very important that you pick yourself up and get going again. I cannot think of any successful millionaire today that has never failed before. That's the reality and it is not the end of the world for your online business.

Integrity Is the Watch Word

Be inspired in selling your products. Do not get intimidated with the problems that you come across while building your online business. Learn from them instead. Ups and downs are just natural for online businesses so you need to get used to them. No matter what happens, continue working on your business and you will surely see how your patience and integrity pay off.

Always continue to prepare for success. "It's not the will to win that matters, everyone has that. It's the will to prepare to win that matters." You need to take time in doing all the necessary preparations for your business. You might need to spend some money for this step, but you should never ever skip it.

Do Not Promise What You Cannot Deliver

If you want to avoid making mistakes, you should never ever promise what you cannot deliver to your clients. You need to gain and earn their trust. In order for you to do that, you need to make sure that you can address their problems and provide solutions to them. Always remember the limitations of your business and stick to them.

Join Likeminded Networks and Surround Yourself with Great MasterMind Team

Find a Free Mastermind Group to Join: Join as a member of an association that has a mastermind network. You may also use the search engines in looking for geographically specific mastermind group. To join my free Mastermind network, please visit <u>VIP Network/MasterMind Group</u> to sign up and download 200 free Business Tools instantly.

Some free mastermind groups are still unpublicized, so you might need to contact them through network groups, chambers of commerce, education centre and lead groups.

Start a NEW Mastermind Group Yourself: If you do not prefer to join a mastermind group, then you may simply create yours. You may just invite some people to join your own group. In that way, you will have control over the group. You will decide who will be allowed to join the group. You will also be the one who will set the goals of the group.

Join a Fee-Based Mastermind Group: Some mastermind groups are free, and some are not. It will make an economic sense if you will join a fee-based mastermind group. You will need to pay from $50 per month or $10,000 a year. Most leading business experts have inspiring mastermind network. If you want to be added in our mastermind network, you may simply send me an <u>e-mail</u>.

In joining a mastermind group, you should expect the members to be highly energetic and result-driven. They are competitive people who want to become successful in business just like you. You need to be as competitive as them.

<u>MeetUp.com</u> is one of the best resources in finding people to get together as a group. If you are really interested in joining a mastermind group, you are free to choose a free one. However, you also have the choice to start your own or join a fee-based one. You will surely thank me for this information later.

Relax and Have Fun

I strongly believe that if you can follow the strategies led down in this book and implement every strategy contained in this book in your Online Business, there is no way you cannot become a successful online business owner. Once you have done everything that you have been taught in this book, it is now time for you to relax and have fun! Do not forget to inspire other aspiring home based online business owners by telling them about this <u>book</u> so they too can <u>benefit from it</u>.

Bonus Gifts

◆ Bonus Gift 1

Download free ebook

http://goo.gl/nBONq

◆ Bonus Gift 2

200 Free Business Tools

http://goo.gl/6muzd

◆ Bonus Gift 3

Free Link Building Ebook

http://goo.gl/orOZ7

Appendices

Your Internet Marketing Road Map

Your Affiliate offer profit channel

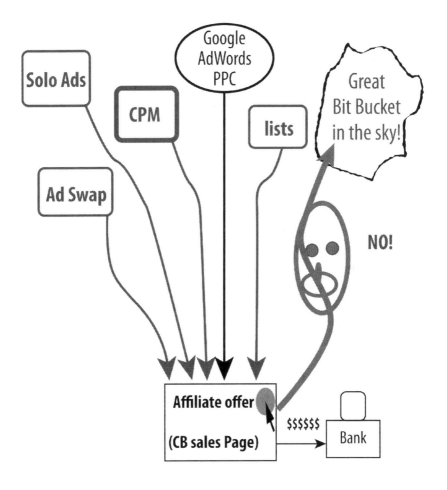

Search engine optimization (SEO)

SEO in order of importance:

1. URL – web address, taken from headline
2. Headline – title of article
3. First paragraph/meta description – Keyword heavy
4. Inbound links – Links from external/internal sites – This is why social bookmarking and blogging are important. Blog about your articles!
5. Keywords in text – Top heavy (first paragraphs)
6. Meta keywords – The hidden keywords

All articles aim to have all these elements.

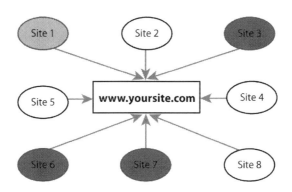

About The Author

Genevieve-Gold Flight (Genevieve Flight) is an Author, Speaker & Online Business Strategist™, a graduate of Open University, UK and an Online Business Entrepreneur. Her passion for transformational leadership, her desire to motivate and inspire others towards starting an online business, led her into deciding to write this book to help both aspiring online business owners and those who currently own an online business. The Secret Code To Success And Wealth™ In Online Business is the first of its kind in her book series and Genevieve is the only Online Business Strategist™ that uses the DiaMonD GiFT ™ Technique for coaching her Clients. Genevieve is a Rotarian and a founding member of several Online Networking Communities which can empower people. She has also spoken at both local and international events. Genevieve currently lives in London and has traveled far and wide around the globe and loves networking, dancing, music and volunteering. You can contact her on +447562642826 or email info@thesecretcodetosuccessandwealth.com and Visit http://www.thesecretcodetosuccessandwealth.com

Made in the USA
Charleston, SC
25 April 2013